PSYCHO PAT
LEGEND OR MADMAN?

PSYCHO PAT
LEGEND OR MADMAN?
PAT VAN DEN HAUWE
MY AUTOBIOGRAPHY

JOHN BLAKE

Published by John Blake Publishing Ltd,
3 Bramber Court, 2 Bramber Road,
London W14 9PB, England

www.johnblakepublishing.co.uk

www.facebook.com/Johnblakepub   facebook

twitter.com/johnblakepub   twitter

First published in hardback in 2012

ISBN: 978-1-84358-754-5

British Library Cataloguing-in-Publication Data:

A catalogue record for this book is available from the British Library.

Design by www.envydesign.co.uk

Printed in Great Britain by CPI Group (UK) Ltd, Croydon, CR0 4YY

1 3 5 7 9 10 8 6 4 2

Papers used by John Blake Publishing are natural, recyclable products
made from wood grown in sustainable forests. The manufacturing
processes conform to the environmental regulations
of the country of origin.

Every attempt has been made to contact the relevant copyright-holders,
but some were unobtainable. We would be grateful if the
appropriate people could contact us.

This book is dedicated to:

My wife, Carolyn, who has stood by my side since June 1996 and supported me through thick and thin and sick and sin. I am so fortunate to have her in my life even though it was touch and go a good many times.

My daughter Gemma – I am so grateful that we eventually had the opportunity to bond as father and daughter, having left her at a very young age.

My extended family – the Everton family – especially the fans who have supported me past and present. My time at 'the People's Club' was without doubt the best days of my life, 100 per cent on and 100 per cent off the field! Thanks for the great memories.

CONTENTS

ACKNOWLEDGEMENTS

Without sounding like a bimbo pop singer collecting a fake gold gong at the MTV awards, I really do need to thank the following people as, without their help, friendship and guidance, there would be no story to tell:

Howard Kendall – thanks for giving me, a Second Division full-back, the chance to play in the big league. I hope I justified the faith you had in me. It was an absolute honour to play for a manager and gentleman such as yourself.

Colin Harvey – nothing much changed besides a few players coming and going, but the respect for Colin has remained, the same as it has for Howard. I regret not taking the improved contract offered to me before my move to Spurs. I really enjoyed working under Colin's management, even though I let him down on the odd occasion – I apologise for that, and thanks for putting up with me!

Terry Venables – a man respected by so many, including myself, even though I went walkies a couple of times! I enjoyed every moment of the three years I worked under Terry and thank him for giving me the opportunity to do so.

Mick McCarthy – when things were not going too well for me he saw something in me and saved me from the scrap heap after a bastard named Ardiles did his best to end my career prematurely. Mick is as straight as they come and, apart from his hair, there are no grey areas! We had our fall-outs but I regard him as a fantastic person. Thanks, Mick – all the best.

Mike England – playing for Wales under Mike was an absolute pleasure. Mike was one of the easiest people I ever had the good fortune of playing for and I say that with the utmost respect and wish him all the very best life has to offer.

Nick Trainer – where do I begin? I'd hate to think where I would be today if it wasn't for this fella. He has been a good friend for many years and I hope we have many more years of the same. Thank you for always being there.

John and Lynne Smith – I have known John, Lynne and the Smith family for a number of years and love and respect them as my own family. I hold them very close to my heart and look forward to seeing them at every opportunity and thank them for always being there for me. Please say hello to all in the Rehab, Lark Lane.

Joe Bennett Snr, Joey Bennett Jnr and family – catching up

with you all after 25 years was a great occasion; we shared a lot of good times back in the day. Could you also say hello to all in the Canfield.

Andy Nicholls – without you, pal, this book would not have been possible. Thanks for all the hard work you have put into this project and for some great laughs along the way ... 'Un-ban the Everton 1!'

Pat

FOREWORD BY HOWARD KENDALL

As I was coming towards the end of my career at Birmingham City, a teenaged London lad was embarking on his and, although I only saw him a few times during training, I thought that even at such a young age he was special. That was in 1977 and, about six years later, I went back to my old club and paid just £90,000 to sign the player who, although still a bit raw, was worth a punt at that kind of money. Hence Pat Van Den Hauwe joined Everton Football Club – it was money well spent!

I had sent my chief scout, Terry Darracott, to have a look at Pat on several occasions and his reports echoed my sentiments that he was a player worth adding to our fast-improving squad at Goodison Park. After a couple of tough seasons, Everton had just won the FA Cup and I believed were in with an excellent chance of competing for honours both at home and in Europe. We had a young, energetic side with one or two older, more experienced players like Peter Reid and Andy Gray helping the less seasoned professionals along the way.

I already had a very good left-back at the club in John Bailey but lacked cover in that area so made the decision to approach Birmingham for Van Den Hauwe. I was fully aware that he had a bad-boy reputation but that probably made the move more likely to go ahead as they were shipping a few players out having been relegated, and most of them seem to have been tagged with a similar image to Pat's. That proved to be the case as, after a tentative enquiry, I was told in no uncertain terms that if I wanted him, I could have him!

We met and discussed terms in a restaurant near my home and I was impressed with his eagerness to play for me. Money was never an issue with Pat and we had a pleasant afternoon. Before I left, we shook hands and, in principle, agreed that he would join us. I wanted the deal to be kept secret as I was worried some other clubs may be sniffing around him so was delighted when I met him in the morning and he reiterated his desire to join us. I did notice he smelled heavily of booze – in fact, he reeked of it – but I decided against ticking him off. If joining a fantastic club like Everton isn't a reason to celebrate with a drink or two, what is?

He turned out to be a far better player than we could ever have imagined and soon I had international managers enquiring about him and, although he opted to play for Wales, I believed he could have represented England and not looked out of place alongside the country's finest players.

Pat was so talented that when he played at centre-half for me when called upon he was often our best player on the pitch, a truly great athlete but also a very talented footballer. I think the 'Psycho' tag was unjustified as he was not a dirty player. Hard and tough, yes – dirty, no.

Of course, off the field he would keep me on my toes; he was a colourful character who loved a social drink and the odd night out. Maybe I am being a little protective of him saying that, but regardless of where he went and what he got up to, come match day he was up for it and never, ever let me down.

During one trip abroad, Pat's antics went a bit far and I was informed by our Chairman, Sir Philip Carter, that the captain of the aircraft had told him that when we landed the police we going to interview the players. Allegedly, one had exposed himself to a stewardess. Once we landed, no player would admit to being the culprit, and no player would point the guilty person out, so we were given a serious ticking off and warned about our future conduct. I was particularly annoyed about this incident as, when we had joined the connecting flight to our final destination, the in-flight bar had been withdrawn!

I met Pat about two years ago at the 'Boys of '85' reunion and he finally admitted that it was he who had flashed at the air stewardess. Over 20 years on, I was in no position to fine him so we had a beer and good laugh about it. It was great to see him after so many years; he still had his film star looks and seemed to be as fit as when he played for me.

I sincerely hope that this project helps to kick start his ventures in South Africa as he has openly told me that he has struggled over the past few years to forge a decent career out there. I have no doubt that things will improve for him, as you can't keep a good man down for long and, believe me, Pat Van Den Hauwe is a good man.

When I look back at every signing I have made at all the clubs I managed, one stands out head and shoulders above any other – Neville Southall. After Neville, I would honestly say that Pat was my second-greatest signing; £90,000 of Everton's money was invested very wisely when Birmingham City cashed that cheque. And given that Pat probably paid the club about half that amount back in fines, it was a very good investment indeed!

Good luck, son, you deserve it.

FOREWORD BY TERRY VENABLES

After a few years in charge of Tottenham, I had assembled a reasonable squad of players that I believed was maybe two or three quality additions short of being capable of challenging for the League title.

One area I needed to strengthen was my defence and I knew that I would require a player who had played at the highest level and Pat came to mind as he had done so at Everton, playing in a Championship-winning team, and was used to competing and succeeding at that level. I also liked the boy's versatility as he was comfortable playing at left or right back and also in the centre of defence.

I was surprised although happy that my enquiry to Everton came back with a positive response and we soon wrapped up the deal to bring Pat back to London.

Although things did not quite work out as well as both of us would have liked, I am pleased that he was a member of my FA Cup winning side in 1991 as he had suffered heartbreak in three previous FA Cup finals with Everton.

Off the field, I knew Pat was a bit of a lad but thought we would be able to work together, and that is how it was. Although he lost his temper sometimes and would give me that evil snarl that frightened so many opponents, he was quick to calm down and didn't bear a grudge. There were a couple of periods when he went missing, but it was a measure of him as a player and a man that he had a conscience and learnt from the problems he caused me as a manager – problems I took full advantage of by going on and on about them to make sure Pat never forgot and never stepped out of line again!

I met Pat in a hotel in London recently and we spoke about his time at Spurs with fondness. I noticed that when he left the meeting he had a tear in his eye, which summed him up. He is a very genuine man, loyal and unaffected by fame.

Good luck, always.

INTRODUCTION

Once you have read my brief introduction you'll probably realise that this book could well be different to the usual ex-footballers' autobiographies that you may have come across. I have tried extremely hard not to clog up the chapters with basic football facts and trivial information about my career. If you need to know how many games I played for Birmingham, Everton, Tottenham Hotspur or Millwall you should have saved your money and just searched on the Internet as statistics really don't float my boat.

I have, with the help of my publicist, tried to make the crazy story of my life as interesting as possible – some years ago, I wrote something along the lines of this story with the help of a media friend in South Africa, but when I read the completed manuscript I dropped the idea. The manuscript covered my life story but it was not how I would have told you about the chaotic way I went about my business on and off the football pitch. The stories were all mine but the way they were written made me think that it was not really how I saw it. It was too correct, too nice, if you like.

Believe me, throughout my life I have done plenty of things that were not nice, but I decided that if this book was ever to be published then the 'not nice' things that have blighted my career – and, indeed, my life in general – needed to be in it. Despite what people have written and said about me I am just a normal bloke who was fortunate enough to make it as a pro footballer; however, with the so-called fame and fortune came trouble and numerous problematic situations which made my life quite colourful.

Of course, this story will cover my football career as well as off-the-field antics as I think I was an OK sort of player, although I was certainly not the greatest professional ever to grace the game. I don't think anybody who I worked with or who watched me would disagree that, on the pitch, I always gave 100 per cent and tried my very best for whichever team I turned out for.

Unfortunately, to be a top professional you need to give 100 per cent in other areas, none more so than when you're training. You need to keep out of the headlines, stay clear of the drink and definitely the drugs. You need to be very careful who you look upon as your close friends and be careful not to mix with the wrong sort of people, people who may get you a bad reputation, lead you astray or who will invariably cause you a few problems. You need to have an open mind and listen to good advice and take your time before making decisions.

Like I said, I gave 100 per cent on the pitch; that, however, was not good enough, as when I look at all the other pointers I have mentioned, I'm honest enough to admit that I failed miserably on all counts. But looking back, apart from one or two huge mistakes I made, I don't think I would have done anything any differently if I had my time again. I sincerely mean that, I really do.

I will have celebrated my 51st birthday by the time this book is launched, and I am in good health with a loving wife and a beautiful daughter, both of whom I adore. What more could I ask for? Money? Don't make me laugh, I have squandered more money than most people could earn in a lifetime but it never made me happy. It paid bills and bought me things I could never have afforded had I worked in a factory or as a lorry driver, but it also paid for things which could have killed me.

There is a famous saying – I'm not sure of the exact words – but it's something like 'a fool and his money are easily parted'. Well, I'll tell you another one: 'Pat Van Den Hauwe and his money can seriously damage your health!'

With that in mind, I am grateful that I am still here to tell you my story. I have been to hell and back thanks to living the 'professional footballer' lifestyle. I have had some great times on and off the pitch, won some of the top trophies in British and European football, played at international level and been all over the world getting paid for doing something I loved with a passion.

Off the field, I have lived the life of a rock 'n' roll star, had houses and cars that you only ever see on the TV and in the glossy magazines and that only so-called 'celebrities' could possibly afford. I have even been in those magazines. On the flip side, I have also been in the gutter, been lower than a snake's belly, been on the brink of suicide and been a split second away from killing a man. So this is no ordinary ex-footballer's autobiography – it's the untold story of Pat Van Den Hauwe, and that means a journey a long way from 'ordinary'!

I am not a criminal or a gangster, just an ex-footballer who chose a few wrong paths throughout his life. I have been labelled a 'legend' after my success at Everton and a 'madman' after numerous, high-profile scrapes that I've got into throughout my life. I think I am neither; maybe once you have read this book, you'll have a better idea if I'm a saint or a sinner … a legend or a madman.

1

LONDON CALLING

At least once a month my wife will wake me up from a nightmare that I often have. It's not just a bad dream but a real situation that I found myself in, a situation that to this day makes me weep.

If you had a few guesses at what would cause me so much trauma, you'd probably come up with a few well-known scenarios: why, for example, did I let Norman Whiteside cut inside and get a shot in on goal that cost Everton the treble? If you think the sight of Whiteside running past me celebrating as I dropped to my knees in despair prevents me from sleeping ... you'd be wrong.

Another favourite might be why I didn't get a grip of Gazza early on in the Cup Final a few years later. Maybe a senior pro like myself or Gary Lineker could have calmed him down and prevented him from making that horrendous tackle, a tackle that left him screaming in agony, one that almost ended his career. Is it the image of Gazza screaming in agony that makes me shout out in my sleep? No, it isn't.

Those of you who know about my personal life are maybe thinking that the nightmare scene involves me walking away from my wife, who was in tears holding my baby daughter as I waved goodbye, leaving them to move in with Mandy Smith? That's a close call as, although I don't have nightmares about it, it does make me weep.

The nightmare is none of those. It is actually an incident that occurred in South Africa a couple of years after I had left England and had become heavily involved in the high life and drug culture that goes hand in hand with it.

I wake up screaming as, in the dream, one feature changes from the actual incident. In the dream, I pull the trigger of the .38 Special I have been carrying around with me for months and blow the head off a gentleman called Steven Kentridge. In real life, although the situation actually occurred, I did not pull the trigger. I let the bloke walk away. It was a decision that probably saved my life ... as well as his.

My recurring nightmare never goes away and I am glad, as it makes me realise how fortunate I am still to have my liberty, and it also makes me realise how becoming involved with guns and drugs can only lead to death and despair. I came so close to committing murder that night that I never want to forget how fortunate I am that I chose not to pull the trigger. Every day when I wake up, that is the first thing that comes into my mind.

Before I got to that crazy stage of my life, I had plenty of other memorable moments on the way. My life was one big fairground ride that never seemed to stop. Some parts of it were good, some bad and some plain stupid. I look back at it now with a smile, the occasional tear and with some fondness but, believe me, it was a ride that at times was destined to crash and it was the excitement of waiting for the crash to happen that prevented me from ever getting off. I love excitement and I doubt there are many people who have been on a similar ride and are still here to talk about it. Luckily, I am.

The ride began when I was born on 16 December 1960 in Dendermonde, a town in Belgium. My father was a Belgian national who met my mother on holiday; she came from London and they fell in love. They ended up going back and forth between their respective homes until they settled in my father's home town where they married and brought into the world two healthy, baby boys, myself and my younger brother Rudy. I left Belgium when I was five years old and have no memories of the place whatsoever. Given what I have been told about how boring Belgium is, maybe that's not such a bad thing!

We moved to Bermondsey – Millwall territory – then settled in Deptford, which was not so much rough as tight knit. I was lucky that my mother's cousins had pubs; Harry and Thomas Cottrell were well known in the area so, despite being a new kid on the block and viewed as a bit of an outsider, it did not take long for the word to get round that we were not a family that could be intimidated easily, or have liberties taken.

I went to a small kiddies' school in Bermondsey, then on to Deptford Park Junior High School, where I started playing football and soon noticed a kid called David Memmitt. He used to do things with a tennis ball that older lads could not do with a football; he had amazing talent and could keep the ball up for hours. All he wanted to do was play for Millwall and he did so at the age of 16. Dave was an amazing player but, obviously, he never made the grade as I have never heard of him since I left school, which is a shame as every club in London wanted him to sign for them. Maybe his loyalty to the local side he adored was blind. Either way, far lesser players than him made it, including yours truly.

I was doing OK and playing for the local side and the school team, but my progress was hindered when I broke my ankle in an accident on a park ride. That was the start of my injury nightmare which plagued me throughout my career. As it turned out, that was not the last time I was sidelined from football due to an incident that was not football related. I spent a couple of months in plaster but made a full recovery and was soon back playing.

We then moved to Kidbrooke, to the Ferrier Estate, one of the new, huge estates that were popping up all over the place in the late 1960s and early 1970s. There was just the one pub – The Watt Tyler – a drinking hole that was frequented by just about every rouge and villain on the estate. It was quite a few years before I stated going in there but it was a pub I always visited when I went home until it eventually shut down in the 1990s.

To say I was not interested in school was an understatement; I despised going there, all I wanted to do was play football and any other sport that could get me out of the classroom. I took up judo, boxing, weightlifting and even squash, a sport that was not really known to anyone at the time.

Quite simply, if there was a sport that got me away from school I'd give it a go, the problem being that they expected me to compete in all these activities ... and attend classes! It was never going to happen so, obviously, I stared bunking off and getting into the usual trouble for non-attendance but, no matter how hard my parents and the teachers tried, I simply did not go. I'd get up in the morning, put my uniform on and head off there, but I very rarely made it through the gates as I'd go to the gym or boxing club; anywhere but school, if the truth be known.

I wasn't roaming the streets causing trouble or being a nuisance to anyone, I just preferred to train than to learn about some way of working out how many degrees a circle contained, how to make something useless out of wood or how to dissect a frog, for fuck's sake! Looking back at it now, I think I made the right choice in concentrating on training, improving my fitness and the various sports I played as those activities were more useful in my later life than any of the things I swerved during school hours. Maybe I should have attended the odd maths lesson as, bearing in mind what I have earned and what I have left, I think somehow the sums just don't add up!

I really enjoyed the boxing and the judo; I used to train

with a friend of mine named Bradley Bellmen. It was nothing serious, just the pads and bags, and I never fought in a bout – I just loved the training. Bradley packed it in when he left school and soon became a heroin addict like so many more kids around at the time. I kept away from the shit that was hitting the streets and really took to judo, where I earned an orange or blue belt before giving it up to concentrate on my football.

I was now playing for a team called Kestrel Rangers. Even though I had been playing for the school team and now the Kestrels as a centre-forward, despite being half decent, I could not have been that special as plenty of my team-mates were going for trials with various London clubs but I never seemed to get the call. One of my team-mates was a lad called Micky who actually captained England Schoolboys. He was an exceptional player but, as is so often the case, that was as far as he went and Micky was another who, despite being the best of our group, never made the step up to the professional game.

Out of nowhere, I was asked to go and train with the schoolboys at Arsenal, a chance that was too good to turn down. What a pain in the arse it turned out to be as my uncle took it upon himself to drive me there every Tuesday and Thursday which, depending on the rush-hour traffic, could take an hour-and-a-half each way. I hated it. I put up with it for a year but it did my head in so I simply stopped going and carried on playing for the Kestrels. My uncle and parents, although disappointed, knew that's how I was and there was no way they could change my mind. Even from an early age, if I did not enjoy doing something, I found the easiest way to deal with it was simply to jack it in.

It was about this time when I met Susan Cross, who was to become Mrs Van Den Hauwe Number One. I was about 14 and very shy – I'd never really had a girlfriend. But Susan was stunning, one of five sisters, who were all very pretty girls and a credit to their parents, so I suppose you could call her my first love.

Apart from the academic side of things, I was enjoying life but soon came across a kid who was older than me and who decided to make my life a misery, a horrible bully called Tony Merriman. By this time, I had started going into the pub, not drinking as such but just for the banter and running the odd errand for the older blokes. It was obvious from day one that Merriman took an immediate dislike to me. This twat would not so much beat me up but bully me in its purest sense – grab me by the hair in front of the other lads, slap me around the head, twist my ear and generally abuse me. He was obviously hoping for a reaction. I made it clear to him that I wanted no trouble, but every time he saw me he would give me grief. He was a horrible person and, in later years, he came very close to regretting making an enemy of me as a teenager.

Eventually, my continual no-show at school came to a head. They were sending letters to the house but I was taking them off the postman and replying to the head teacher pretending to be my mother, until one day I came unstuck. On the sorriest day of my life to date, I had to endure the embarrassment of my father marching me through the school gates while everyone was leaving.

A teacher called Mr Adhern took me under his wing and, although he was a rough-and-ready type of bloke, deep down he was a very compassionate man. The kids were not afraid of him but respected him as he wasn't a bully. Remember, in those days teachers could knock the shit out of you, and many did, with no comebacks. Mr Adhern, although more than capable of doing that, just had a presence that made you respect him. He warned me that if I did not toe the line, I'd be sent to a special school but, as I was not really causing trouble, he tried tremendously hard and succeeded to a certain extent to rehabilitate me back into the educational system. When it came to the final year and the exams, I simply did not bother and I left school without a single qualification so, although I respected him, I let him down badly. He was the first but certainly not the last person I let down.

Before I had to look for a way of earning a living, I was offered a trial at Chelsea and that probably saved me from a life of either mundane jobs or crime. Sometimes, when I look back at my life, maybe I would have been better off turning down Chelsea and going down the same route as that of most of my mates. We were shown round Stamford Bridge and even went into the dressing rooms where we saw Ray Wilkins blow-drying his hair wearing just a towel.

We did a full tour of the ground and, well over an hour later, as we arrived back near the dressing rooms, I asked if I could nip back in there as I desperately needed a piss. I walked in and Wilkins was still there in front of the mirror, in his towel, blow-drying his hair. Now, I am no expert in hairdressing, but later on in my life I married quite a famous young lady who was very keen to look her best. I swear to this day she never took as long doing her hair as Wilkins did that day. Looking at him now, maybe he over-cooked his barnet a bit!

After the trials, I was taken on as a youth trainee but had not signed anything and there were an awful lot of young lads in the same boat as me, so I knew I would have to dig deep and work hard to impress. Life at Chelsea was tough; we would play other clubs around London and I was under the watchful eye of Dario Grady, who was to make a very good name for himself within the game, especially when it came to spotting young lads and bringing them through the ranks.

Dario was not the only person on the staff with an eye on the lads, though, and I took a dislike to one of the coaches who seemed to be a bit too friendly, if you get my drift. This fella, who was a giant of a geezer, used to drive us about everywhere in a clapped-out club minibus and get us doing all the shitty jobs around the ground.

One day he told me he needed to show me the games room that the first team players frequented that was situated high up in the new stand that had recently been built. We went up in the lift and I got a feeling that he was standing a bit too close to me and when we got in the games room for the life of me I did not know why he had taken me there. I made some excuse and made a quick exit and was so upset by the bloke's presence I even told my father about him.

He told me to steer well clear and I did, but soon after I was told that, despite trying as hard as I could, Chelsea had decided that I was not good enough and I was released with about a dozen others. We were quite simply told that Chelsea had too many players our age and that we were no longer required to turn up the following day. I was upset but glad to see the back of the coach who, a few years later, was bombed for possessing so-called 'indecent material', so maybe my instincts were correct and it was me he fancied, not a game of pool or table tennis.

Chelsea's rejection made me realise that football was a ruthless game. I would hazard a guess that that day finished some of my team-mates' football careers for good. Luckily for me, I was given a chance elsewhere; sadly, not everybody would get that chance.

Due to my lack of education, football and a few boxing and judo moves was all I knew so it made me more determined to not give up. I was so relieved when I was asked if I'd like to join four of the other lads who had been released and travel to Birmingham with a view to joining them as an apprentice on a one-year deal.

I did not really want to up sticks and leave London – I was still a kid – but I was realistic enough to realise that, after binning Arsenal off and getting bombed from Chelsea, my options were limited. I went home and told my mum and dad that I was packing my bags and leaving home. It was heartbreaking both for me as well as my parents and plenty of tears were shed when I walked out the door to embark on a truly amazing journey.

They gave me what spare cash they had to tide me over until I got paid, although I'm not sure if they would have been so upset had they realised that, 15 years later, I would return to the same home after my journey had come full circle with less money in my pocket than they had given me when I'd left.

2

BOUNCING BACK

I arrived in Birmingham on 8 June 1977 with a sports holdall containing my boots and a few items of clothing and about a tenner in my pocket thanks to my parent's generosity. Four lads joined me on the journey from Chelsea to Birmingham and two of them, Paul Ivey and Mark Dennis, like myself, eventually signed professional forms at St Andrew's.

We were met by a gentleman called Alan Gilbert Instone, the club secretary, and signed an 18-month apprentice agreement in the presence of my father. My basic wages were £16 a week but I was promised in the contract 'win and draw bonuses in competitions where the rules of the competition so provide' and also reasonable travel expenses on authorised journeys! So the ride had begun.

The first team manager at the time was Willy Bell and, just a couple of months into my apprenticeship, he summoned me to his office and said that it was his opinion that I was not going to make the grade. I had not set eyes on the fella previously, apart from when we were sweeping the dressing rooms out, but pleaded with him to give me another chance. He muttered something about discussing it with the coaching staff but the following day he was sacked – much to my delight! He never worked in football again and ended up as a religious preacher, so what does that tell you about his football knowledge?

Sir Alf Ramsey took over from Bell but I had no dealings with him whatsoever and just carried on training with the youth team under Keith Bradley. I was doing OK but the club were rocked when Alf resigned after a big row broke out involving Trevor Francis. We were all told that after initially accepting Trevor's transfer request, the board changed their minds, fearful they would 'incur the wrath of already disgruntled fans', so Ramsey duly handed in his notice.

I don't know if Ramsey had a problem with Francis or if it was the other way around, but apparently he had recommended that both Trevor and central defender Joe Gallagher should be transfer-listed. Both were big favourites with the crowd; indeed, Francis was already a legend at St Andrew's. Trevor was a fantastic player so obviously it would upset the crowd if he was allowed to leave, more so than if Ramsey went, which turned out to be the case. The situation was obviously down to Trevor as he left the following season anyway.

Such matters were no concern of mine and I just carried on training hard in the hope I would get my chance to impress. I had only been at the club ten months and when Jim Smith was appointed he was the third manager to cast his eye over me. Some of the training staff were taking a shine to me and one in particular nicknamed me 'The Stallion'. Believe me, at that stage of my life, it was due to my fitness during training and nothing else!

I began to watch a player who, from the first time I set eyes on him, made me realise that I had so much to learn. Colin Todd was coming towards the end of his career but was pure quality. The way he read the game was world class and I studied the way he played the game and tried to copy his style, which was not easy, as he was an unbelievable player.

Jim Smith lasted longer than my previous two bosses and, during the 1978–79 pre-season training he began involving me and few other youngsters, including my mate Mark Dennis, with first team sessions. Mark was always in with a chance of making the grade because, as well as being a decent footballer, he was that fast he could catch pigeons. Smith told us all that there were places up for grabs and that if we trained hard and played well in the reserves we would get our chance. Mark and my good self were then selected to go on the first-team pre-season tour to Spain and I played against some Spanish side and did really well. As we were coming off the pitch, Smith put his hand out and congratulated me on my performance but, before I had chance to thank him, a bottle was thrown from the crowd and landed on my head which spoiled the moment somewhat!

Jim was true to his word and Mark Dennis made his début at the start of the season and, a few weeks later, both of us were selected to play against Manchester City on 14 October 1978. Allegedly, it was in an edition of the *Guinness Book of Records* that Mark and I were the youngest pairing full-backs to play at the same time in a top-flight fixture. However, I bet the record books don't mention that it was one of the worst débuts ever and the most horrendous day of my young life to date.

I was up against Peter Barnes, the England left-winger, who showed me no mercy as he took me to the cleaners. He totally took the piss and even nutmegged me twice in the game that ended in a 2–1 win for Man City, although I was dragged off long before the final whistle when the boss put me out of my misery. And in all honesty, he would have been within his rights to shoot me – that would have been better than facing Barnes any longer.

It was indeed a début from hell, although what came next was soul-destroying. In the dressing room, Jim Smith went absolutely berserk at us all and started swearing and throwing tea cups at the wall. He then picked me out, in what I remember as the worst moment of my career. I will never forget his words; he pointed at me and said, 'You, you fucking useless cunt, get changed … you'll never wear this kit again.'

He then went on to say I'd not only let him down, but every one of the lads in the team, and it hurt me for quite a while. I was distraught. I think Smith was poor doing that, his man-management skills were not the best. Surely an arm around me and a 'get your head up, son …' would have worked better. It took me a long, long time to recover from that incident; my confidence was at an all-time low.

It was six months before I got another game and, by then, we were as good as relegated and Smith decided to give a few reserves a run out. I had never been so nervous in my life as I knew that, if I played as badly again, I'd be finished. Luckily enough, I did well and played out the last few games, although I think Smith had seen enough of me as a left-back as I played just about everywhere else on the pitch. Of all the positions I played, I think I was best as sweeper; I was no Colin Todd, but I felt comfortable there. Maybe it was because you didn't have to do much running!

I only played one game during the 1979/80 season, against Fulham, and it was another nightmare as I was injured when I went up for a header, landed awkwardly and jarred my back. I carried on the best I could but from 3–0 up we lost 3–4. Back in the dressing room, the manager started having a go but took one look at me and shut up; he could see I was in a bad way as I was walking like a zombie and could not even bend down to take my boots off. Maybe I should have asked to come off but after Fulham began to get back into the game, I didn't want people to think I was trying to escape out of the firing line, so to speak. Maybe the manager should have clocked that I was struggling; had he subbed me, I would have gladly come off. As it was, neither of us made the decision and it was the lack of communication between us that almost blew the whistle on my football career before it had kicked off.

My condition was going down hill rapidly and I was unable to walk at all after a few minutes, so the lads carried me into the shower and washed me down, helped me to get dressed and I was taken straight to hospital where I an X-ray revealed that I had dislodged a disc from my spine. It was not a straightforward slipped disc but far more serious and, after some treatment, I was put into an upper-body cast. It was the most uncomfortable thing you could ever imagine having to wear. The contraption was heavy, hot and itched like the worst case of crabs imaginable. There was a cut-out to allow your stomach to expand but food and drink were the last thing on my mind as I shuffled about looking like something out of a horror film.

I had to stay in the cast for almost two months and stay completely still. It did my head in so I went back to London and stayed with my parents until the cast was removed and I began a long, hard road back to recovery. The doctors warned me that it would be a lengthy process as the disc could move again, as once something like that had been injured it would never be the same again. I had to take every day at a time and it was months before I could jog, let alone run or participate in any training that involved physical contact. Without me, the lads did great and we were promoted back to the top flight having finished third in the league.

Both I and the club knew that it was a serious injury, a possible career-threatening one, but I don't think anyone thought that I would be out for nearly two seasons with it. I was a very fit young man and that helped me immensely. As it was, it took from August 1979 to April 1981 before I made my comeback as a substitute during a home game against Crystal Palace.

The problem with back injuries is that it is a truly complex part of your body. If you break your leg, the medical staff can look at the X-ray and tell you roughly within a month or two when you will return to action. With serious back injuries, they cannot do that and, although I felt about 90 per cent right, there was a niggle in the back of my mind that had me wondering whether I was ready to play again.

I discussed it with the gaffer and we agreed I'd give it a go. The ground was empty with less than 10,000 in attendance, but it could have been played before one man and his dog and it would still have felt like I was running on to the pitch before 100,000 at Wembley, such was my delight to be back on the pitch.

Those 20 months on the sidelines seemed like 20 years. It

was a horrendous part of my career and, had it not been for the support of my team-mates, the management and the backroom staff at St Andrew's, I'd probably never have played again. As it was, I played in the next couple of games and felt OK, not fully fit, just OK, but in my third game back at Leicester City the injury flared up again and I wondered if I was finished and that all the hard work had been a waste of time.

I was back in hospital and met a specialist who put my mind at rest, telling me that although the injury was connected to the original problem, once again I just needed to rest and that I would eventually regain full fitness. For once in my life, I took the advice of those who knew best and let the injury clear up until I felt no discomfort at all. I felt I was ready to start playing when we all returned to pre-season training and was frustrated when I was overlooked for the opening games. The boss was right, though, and he knew that if I was not 100 per cent match fit then I could be out for months again, so we took things nice and steady and I made my first start away at Old Trafford before 48,000 fans and played OK at right-back in a creditable 1–1 draw. I was ecstatic.

I was covering for the first-choice right-back Davie Langan who was out injured but I must have impressed Jim Smith as I secured a starting place, although it was at right- and left-back, centre-half, sweeper and even the odd cameo performance in midfield. By now, I was getting on with Jim Smith, who had seemed to have taken to me and we got on well. He was not my idea of a good man-

manager, but off the field he was a superb bloke and we had some good times together so I was sad when he and the club parted company.

It was a shock when the board appointed Ron Saunders to replace Smith, as he had only just walked out on local rivals Aston Villa some two weeks earlier. His first game in charge should have been against Villa, a game scheduled for the Saturday, but either he or the club bottled it as he took over formally as manager the following Monday after we had lost 1–0. I kept my place under Saunders and, although as a team we struggled and finished just above the drop zone, I was offered a new, improved contract and signed it without hesitation, partly because I was just happy to be playing and partly to repay the people at the club for helping me recover from the dreadful injury nightmare I had been through. Saunders was a decent manager and I thought the following season could be a great one for both myself and Birmingham City.

In reality, it was a bit of a non-event and we never really improved from the previous season; there were some highs and plenty of lows. I was dropped after the first five games when we contrived to concede 17 goals in just 4 of them and also missed a few games with an injury unrelated to my back problems. On my return, I scored my only goal for the Blues in the game against Arsenal at St Andrews, although it was a pity there were only 11,276 there to see it. I was playing in midfield and found myself in space when Kevin Dillon put a superb through-ball in behind their back four. I raced on to it and was one-on-one with the 'keeper and I shit myself. I had never been in this situation before so I simply put my head down, took the ball a few paces and smashed it as hard as I could with my right foot. It flew into the bottom corner and I was as shocked as everyone else. Arsenal went up other end and equalised but Dillon then got a second and we held on for a win.

I played quite a few games in midfield after the Arsenal game, one being a home fixture against Spurs. During the first half, I went in hard on Ozzie Ardiles and he was rolling around on the ground squealing like a baby. I stood over him and told him he was a whining Argie bastard and to get up. It was a comment that years later came back and bit me on the arse big time.

After the departure of Mark Dennis in the following close-season, the number 3 shirt was given to me but, after a good pre-season, any early optimism that we would do well was blown away with a 4–0 opening-day defeat by West Ham and we were right to fear the worst – that it would be a long, hard campaign.

Most things about this season were largely forgettable. I was an ever-present and we were not a bad side but lost too many games by the odd goal – an amazing14 in total. There were definitely worse teams than us in the division; Mick Harford was a quality striker, Tony Coton a top 'keeper, but it was another false dawn for the Blues and, despite a win against the Villa and closing the season with three draws, the trap-door opened and we again dropped to Division 2.

I was as gutted as the rest of the lads but, at the time, did not know that I would be back in the top division sooner than I thought.

3

CRAZY GANG WARFARE

As soon as I arrived in Birmingham, I was put in digs with Paul Ivey and we were looked after by a nice elderly couple who we nicknamed George and Mildred. Both Paul and I found it hard – we were homesick and had little spare cash, I was so skint my parents used to send me money as well as food parcels, as I was not being fed as much as I was used to either.

George used to drive us round in his clapped-out, blue Robin Reliant; it was embarrassing but he was a top fella and he loved taking us to his friends' houses as even though we were only apprentices he felt privileged as a Blues fan that he had potential first-team players living under his roof.

After training, Mark Dennis and I would meet up, have some dinner and drink endless pints of blackcurrant and lemonade while we took on all the other lads in darts competitions in Birmingham City's sports club. We both became very good darts players and we began going into local pubs and playing regulars for money. With not drinking alcohol and practising every afternoon, we won more often than we lost before people began to suss us out and blokes stopped playing us. We had to start hanging around different pubs with a pint of beer in our hands before locals would take us on. It was a great way to top our apprentice money up.

I was a fit lad and found the training quite easy but, at times, it could get a little intimidating as there were fall-outs between so-called team-mates on a regular basis. One such occasion was when two centre-halves, Joe Gallagher and Pat Howard – whom we had just bought from Newcastle – squared up to each other. They were huge blokes compared to us kids and fell out over something or other and, as they were arguing, Joe headbutted Pat and broke his nose and they ended up having a quite serious punch-up. It wasn't nice to see two team-mates fight like that as a young pro, but I soon got used to it.

There always seemed to be unrest where Joe Gallagher was concerned and I remember him having another fall-out with my pal Mark Dennis a few years later when Joe accused Mark of tipping off the press that Gallagher had set up a move to Aston Villa. It was a controversial topic – they were our hated rivals – and when it went pear-shaped, Joe blamed Mark for some reason. It was no surprise to anyone that when Alf Ramsey left, Gallagher was one of the players involved in the bust up.

The first two years were all about growing up and getting to know each other and then when we signed professionally we were allowed to find our own digs, so I moved in with a gentleman called Brian Rogers who was connected with the club and owned a huge house in which he let rooms to four or five of us. Unlike George and Mildred's, which was more like a boarding school, this move gave us plenty of freedom, which was not a good thing in my case as I soon began making the most of it!

Brian was the manager of a nightclub called Faces and that was the turning point of my time at Birmingham as I began to hit the town. Most nights, I'd be in Faces and I soon got my confidence with the women as Brian knew everyone worth knowing. It was nothing mental – we used to have a few beers, chat the birds up and go for a curry, normal lads' stuff. The problem was, I wasn't an electrician or a student. I was now a professional footballer who had to train the following morning.

Brian was a great guy and loved the women; his wife was always in my ear trying to get me to grass him up and it was a great learning curve for me and I got to know how to duck and dive during my time with him. He sadly died from cancer when I was at the top of my game and I fondly remember him as someone who helped me along the way.

I eventually went to live with Kevin Dillon who had a

house opposite one Mark Dennis had bought and, when he moved on, I bought it from him and joined Mark as a homeowner. Susan used to come up for the weekend but by now I had plenty of girls in tow in town and, more often than not, I'd leave her in Dill's house while I went out with a local bird. Dill used to tell me I was bang out of order, which I was, but it made no difference and I carried on regardless.

I became a regular at Faces and got friendly with some lads called Alan and Peter McAteer, and another lad nicknamed Kimo, who I became best mates with. I was with some of the football lads one night at the club and, for some stupid reason, took my shirt off and was dancing around acting the fool when the bouncers came and told me to put it back on. Knowing Brian, I told them to fuck off, and they grabbed me and gave me a good old-fashioned leg and a wing, throwing me across the room head first. I landed on my chin, splitting it open.

I went home covered in blood, told the brothers, who soon assembled a small firm and we went back to the club and knocked on the door. But the doormen shit themselves and would not come out. That night, I knew that the people I was mixed up with were the proper heads and not to be messed with and, from then on, the door staff stayed away from me.

At 17 I bought my first car, a 2-litre Cortina, and used to drive it all over town without a licence. One night I got nicked for speeding so I had a court appearance coming up and was that worried I confided in Frank

Worthington, who kindly agreed to drive me to court to face the music.

Before I went in front of the magistrates, he said, 'If you want to act like a man, be a man and take your punishment' I was in awe of Frank and would go along with just about anything he said, so in I went and was given a hefty fine which I paid, although I did not bother getting a licence and kept on driving afterwards.

By the time I was 18, a gang of us started to frequent a very well hidden pub called the 'Odd Spot' where a barmaid named Jill worked. She was 34 and quite pretty and soon we started talking and getting on well. Over a few weeks, it was just me going to the pub to talk with Jill and soon we were shagging each other's brains out. For the five months we were together, all we did was shag, including a record seven times from a Saturday night to the Sunday afternoon.

Jill used to drop me off at training and soon Jim Smith clocked that she was way older than me and began telling me I should keep away from her because I was too fucked to train on the Monday due to all the shagging we were doing. He had a point!

Frank Worthington had taken a shine to me and we began going out and usually I was driving. One night I was getting ready to go out with him to a club called Liberties when he opened a compartment in his wardrobe and took out a small pipe. He then proceeded to fill it with weed and began smoking it before telling me once again it was my turn to drive. En route, Frank asked me if I would like to take a puff from this pipe, which I did, and we eventually got to the club even though I could hardly see. Once inside Liberties, Frank went about his business regarding the birds, while I sat slumped in a seat not knowing what day it was.

I got involved with another firm called the Bagshaws and they seemed nice enough but one night I was in bed with Susan when we were awoken by the sound of someone trying to get into the house. I got hold of a replica gun that the Bagshaws had given me and caught the intruder in the garden and pointed the gun at him and said that if he moved I was going to shoot the fucker, but he just walked off laughing. A few weeks later when we went to London during the pre-season break, I asked Kimo to keep an eye on my house but when I got back it had been burgled – by the Bagshaws. I often wondered if it had been one of their firm a few weeks previously who had tried to screw the house, and knew the gun they had given me was a replica!

Before long, Susan moved in with me full time but one night she got the hump and buggered off for a week. Given my single man status back, I set about enjoying myself and Kimo brought two sisters back to my place for a private party. We were having a great time drinking and watching pornos when, out of the blue, Susan came back. I heard the front door go so I ran into the hall and slammed it on her and she bit my finger as I was trying to stop her getting into the house. During this time, my dog – a huge Doberman – escaped. When the girls eventually got out and Susan had calmed down, I went looking for the dog and, before long, found it sitting outside the pub I frequented most nights.

Soon we had our own little firm at the club who were nicknamed locally 'The Brummie Bashers'. We were also called 'The Magnificent Seven' and, regardless of what other people called us, we were most certainly the original Crazy Gang – myself, Noel Blake, Mark Dennis, Robert Hopkins, Tony Coton, Mick Harford, Howard Gayle and the legendary Frank Worthington were all good mates and, although Frank was not really a member of the gang when it began to hit the local papers, he was a founder member who was always good company to be out with and the fun and trouble we all got are indeed as legendary as Frank.

During a pre-season tour in Scandinavia, we were staying in one of those shitty complexes tucked away in the middle of nowhere. With no nightlife to speak of, the lads set me up with a bird who worked as a waitress. I got her back to my room, which contained little kiddie-style bunk beds – with Birmingham, it was never a case of no expense spared – so I climbed on to the top bunk with the waitress and just as I was about to do the deed all the lads were outside looking directly at us through the window. All the usual suspects we there laughing their heads off, so the bird got dressed, jumped off the bunk and fucked off, never to be seen again.

On the same tour we were in a pub when what I believe was a transvestite latched on to me. He or she came up to me and we had a drink and a chat and, for the life of me, I could not make my mind up if it was a bloke, a woman or a 50/50! He/she said they needed somewhere to sleep and was all over me so, before I invited him/her back to the hotel, I asked them to go to the toilets for a check out. This thing went straight into the gents, which got my alarm bells ringing. So I followed to see what was down below. Off came the knickers and, although there was no visible problem as there was not a cock in sight, I was still unsure, so binned him/her off. I was lucky that I had bumped into them early doors as, if I had been pissed, I may have not been as alert and made a big mistake.

On another tour to South America we had to wait for our connecting flight and, by the time we were due to board the plane, we were well and truly pissed. I became friendly with some girl and we got chatting but, being half pissed, I got my dick out. Unknown to me, there were casually dressed security guards patrolling the departure lounge who quickly arrested me and put me in a lock-up in the airport, saying they were going to deport me back to the UK. Jim Smith was notified and he came and spoke to the officials telling them to keep me there. Without telling me, Smith had asked an official to keep me in there to teach me a lesson, and then release me five minutes before my flight – which they did. I had to leg it to my connecting plane and boarded with my head bowed in shame as the lads chanted all sorts of obscenities about me.

When we eventually settled on the tour, we were messing

about around the pool when a club official asked me to come out with him to look for some women. On the way, he said I was not going to play the next day so we went to a brothel for a few drinks and had a good laugh as we knocked back a few whiskies, the drink favoured by the official. We ended up taking the bait and went upstairs with a couple of birds and got into a room with two and began getting our money's worth. He was on one bed while I was on other when, all of a sudden, his hooker started yelling, 'No ... no ... too big!' He jumped off the bed and shouted, 'What kind of a fucking knocking shop is this?'

Before he pissed off he told me to come with him but we had paid up front so I told him I'd see him back at the hotel. Once I got back, he had a right strop on and was calling me all sorts. The following day, he had sorted it so I had to play as pay-back for me getting my money's worth and him losing his.

A few of us quite often frequented a local brothel after training where we could buy some booze, talk to the birds, have a sauna and, if needs must, have a dabble with the girls. One of them came downstairs after being with one of the lads saying that she had never had such a treat in her life, although I believe she still charged my well-endowed team-mate full price!

We also used to visit a mixed sauna, but you had to wear swimming gear. One day, I got talking to a girl for about half-an-hour and I hinted I was off for a shower and she took the wink and followed me. We were soon bang at it but got a bit noisy and some of the older guests weren't very happy about it. A few minutes later, we were politely asked to leave and told never to come back.

Back on the road, I was driving as usual without a licence having had a few drinks with my team-mate Les Philips. One night, we had a couple of birds in the back of the car and were going from pub to pub when we approached a huge roundabout in the centre of Birmingham. I asked the girl in the back for directions but she had no idea where we were going, so I got the hump and carried on going round and round this huge roundabout. Eventually, she yelled that if I did not stop she was going to jump out, so I carried on doing it. Then on the third or fourth lap the silly cow opened the door and dived out while we were still circling. I calmly carried on driving and slowed down to check if she was all right, saw that she was, so stopped and let her mate get out before we carried on to the next pub.

I was out with Mick Harford and our partners on another barmy night. We had been on our best behaviour, had enjoyed a nice meal and a couple of drinks and were travelling home when these four idiots decided to cut us up on the road. Mick had never had the mildest of tempers so the chase began! We were in pursuit of this car for at least ten minutes, tailing it all over Birmingham. Eventually, Mick cut them off and stopped in front of their car before calmly getting out, joined by myself. They seemed up for it so I asked Mick what he was going to do as, by now, although they had stayed in their car they were effing and blinding at us and generally taking the piss. Mick calmly opened his boot which, coincidently, contained his golf clubs, and selected the heaviest one out of his collection. He then walked up to the car and started smashing it up! First the windscreen, then the headlights and, as he went for the driver's door, they got out of the car and ran down the road. Mick finished the car off and we got back in and drove off as if nothing had happened. There were repercussions as the club was notified, and Mick had to pay for the damages or face prosecution.

Similar to spending time with Mick, there was never a dull moment when out with Mark Dennis and his wife Jane. On one occasion, we went to a club in Solihull and had a good night but, as we were leaving, an argument began and it was Jane instead of Mark fighting as she ploughed into three girls. Jane could fight like a man and floored the biggest one when she kicked her in the groin. I heard the bone crack and the girl fell to the floor, so we left rather quickly.

On another occasion we were at Mark's house for a party with a few players and he had an English bull terrier called Charlie. The music was playing yet we still heard a loud, screeching, high-pitched sound. Jane opened the back door to see what was going on only to find out that the noise was coming from next door's cat that Charlie had just ripped to shreds. The next-door neighbour then naturally went mental, so we left the party just as Mark and Jane started fighting, which, like I said, was the same as two men going at it with each other.

Alan Curbishley was a quiet bloke but he had a brother-in-law who managed The Who. Curbs sorted us all out with tickets and, prior to the gig, we were taken backstage for drinks and to meet the band. The dressing room was full of the usual birds and drink but I noticed a table covered in funny-looking 'Smarties' which was an eye-opener for us all. Curbs' brother-in-law asked whether I'd like to go out on stage for a look and it was amazing. In a football ground, even when it's a full house, the fans are on four sides of you; here there were literally thousands of people just staring at you and it scared me shitless. I went back to the dressing room and they were dishing the pills out; I wasn't surprised, for if they had asked me to go on and play the triangle for 30 seconds, I'd have had to take the fuckers as well.

Despite being regarded as a crazy and fearsome group of lads, we decided to give one potential trouble spot a wide berth while on a tour in Peru. We had been given a day off training and a group of us went for a walk to a very busy, open-air market. As we were nosing about looking at various stalls full of junk, I felt a sharp pain around my neck and shouted out to Keith Birchen who was nearby to help me. My solid gold chain with the letter 'P' hanging from it had gone and there was blood all over my hand where I had felt my neck.

My first reaction was that some fucker had cut me, so we all went back to the hotel where I looked in the mirror to find I had three deep cuts around my neck. I got the club physio to clean it up and it was not as bad as it had looked.

It was a very shady place with no end of dark passageways and, by now, it was pitch dark, so despite being somewhat crazy, we decided we were not crazy enough to go looking for the thief who had yanked my chain. Literally!

4

OUT OF THE BLUE ... AND OVER THE MOON

So Birmingham were back in the Second Division but our season had got off to a flyer as we won five on the trot before losing at home to Pompey in a feisty mid-week encounter. We always had a day off after a game so, on the Thursday, we assembled in training and were gathered in the usual circle chatting and flicking the ball about waiting for the gaffer to show and begin the inquest into our recent defeat. After about half-an-hour, we were getting restless; the boss was never usually late but, eventually, Ron turned up and told us all to listen carefully as he had just come from a meeting with the club chairman and unfortunately two players had to leave the club immediately.

We all looked at each other in shock. There had been a clear-out pre-season and we all thought that was the end of it as some of the snippets that had appeared in the press about the reputation some of us had in and around town were directed at a couple of the lads shipped out in the summer. Although we had dropped a division, it did not have the same impact as it does today. The wages players were on in the 1980s weren't massive and were manageable even when most clubs suffered relegation.

There was no major TV money keeping clubs afloat; ITV or BBC showed the odd game and probably paid a couple of grand for the privilege. Home gates maybe dropped by a couple of thousand, but sponsorship deals with some local brewery or car dealer were not dependant on top-flight football, so if players were getting transferred without asking for a move there was usually an internal issue behind it.

We stood in the circle and most of us had our heads bowed. I don't think any of us were unhappy at the club; of course, we wanted to be playing in Division One, as it was then, but we had got off to a great start and were favourites in many quarters to go straight back up.

Ron got straight to the point and blamed the fact that he had to sell players on the dire financial situation the club was in. To this day, I have no idea if he was telling the truth or covering up the fact that the men in suits were unhappy with our so-called 'behaviour' in town.

He looked at Kevin Dillon and said, 'Watford have come in for you and we have accepted their offer of £250,000 – get your stuff, you're out of here!' It was ruthless and Kev just turned and walked back to the changing rooms in total shock. Saunders then looked directly at me and I thought, 'Oh fuck!'

I loved it at Birmingham; I was playing every week, had settled into a nice house and, although the Magnificent Seven were down to the last couple, I saw that as a chance to put down some roots with my fiancée Susan. Something else I wondered was: who the fuck wants to sign me? It seemed that whoever they were, refusing to join them was not an option. I just took a deep breath and preyed that whoever had put an offer in for me were not in a lower league than Birmingham, or even a poxy club that I knew I would not want to join.

Saunders just pointed at me and said, 'You ... we have accepted an offer of £90,000 ... from Everton Football Club ...'

He probably said a bit more along the lines of 'we are sorry to lose you ...' etc., but I never heard a word of it. My head was buzzing – Everton Football Club, the FA Cup Winners, playing in Europe, a massive club who were in with a chance of winning the Championship. I was off to the dressing room to pack my stuff before Saunders called me back and told me I was to go straight home as Howard Kendall was going to phone me within the hour.

I had watched Everton win the FA Cup on TV just a few months earlier when they beat Watford 2–0. I believed that was a final we could have been in but for John Barnes and Nigel Callahan tearing us apart in the quarter-final. Both those wingers had been marked out of the game by the two

Everton full-backs at Wembley so I began to wonder what the fuck they wanted *me* for.

I rushed home and told Susan the good news. I'm not sure she saw it that way, as she had not long joined me in the Midlands having recently moved up from London where she had lived all her life. Now she would have to pack her bags and move again to Merseyside and, although it may seem selfish, I never discussed it with her. I basically told her we were going. Had she said she didn't want to, I'm afraid it would have been goodbye, as this was a chance of a lifetime and there was no way on earth I was passing on it.

The phone call came and I was told to get a train to Lime Street Station where I would be met by a club official and driven to meet the manager. I was expecting to be driven to Goodison or the training ground, Bellfield, but was taken to a restaurant in Formby to be greeted by a buoyant Howard Kendall. We had a superb afternoon and enjoyed an excellent meal and a glass of wine before he told me that I was going to be taken to a hotel and undertake a medical the following day before being introduced to the press and my new team-mates.

I was on cloud nine and I quite simply could not believe this was happening to me. When Ron Saunders had pointed at me just a few hours earlier, I was thinking that by now I would be somewhere like Notts County or Luton haggling over wages but, instead, I was in the company of a fantastic, up-and-coming, young manager poised to join one of the country's biggest clubs.

Once we finished the meal, Mr Kendall briefly discussed

terms with me and told me that the following day, when I passed the medical, I would be offered a three-year deal. The money on offer was good, probably double what I was on at Birmingham, and I was also offered £25,000 to sign. There were bonuses for winning games and for finishing at various places in the league – it was a fantastic deal.

Had Howard informed me that there was no signing-on fee and I was going to be on the same money as I was getting at St Andrew's, I'd have still asked him for the pen and signed there and then. I felt at home in his company, he had won my trust and total respect over one meal, and he has that to this day.

When he left I got talking to the bar manager, ordered a few drinks and got on the phone to tell everyone my good news. My mother and father were really pleased for me although Susan was still in a state of shock with the speed of the move. I sat back, ordered a bottle of champagne and a few large brandies, then finished the night off with huge, big fat cigar, thinking, 'Fuck me, I have won the jackpot!' I ended up, not for the last time on Merseyside, having a few too many drinks and the restaurant manager eventually got me into a taxi and sent me off to the hotel.

The following day I had the medical and passed with ease, met a few local press reporters and was shown around the training facilities and introduced to Howard's staff who were preparing for a game against Southampton.

I was then introduced to my new team-mates and every one of them seemed quite happy with my arrival – apart from a certain John Bailey, who had obviously noticed that

I played in the same position as him. I went to shake his hand and he blanked me and later that night in the hotel I read in the local paper that when they had asked Bailey whether he thought that Pat Van Den Hauwe had been brought in to replace him, he said, 'Pat who?'

After the blank at Bellfield and then a dig in the press, I thought, 'Fuck you,' and began to think I would have an enemy at the club. I could not have been any further off the mark as, within a few days, Bails had come round and right until his last day at the club he remained one of my closest friends at Everton.

Although Bails already had the hump with me, it had not actually been mentioned where Mr Kendall had intended playing me. I was just happy to sign the form and not cock anything up, so once that was all sorted and the formalities were over, I asked him bluntly where he saw me fitting into his side. I thought it could be as a central defender but he shook his head and said, 'You're my new left-back, although it may be a while before you're my first-choice left-back!' In one sentence, in seconds, he had taken me to the top of the mountain and rolled me back down to the bottom of it. He was a genius at that ... the king of the one-liner!

That day I watched from the stands as my new team struggled to overcome a decent Southampton side and the game ended two each. I went to the players' lounge and Mr Kendall asked me what I fancied to drink. I was obviously on my best behaviour so politely asked for an orange juice. He grinned and said, 'An orange juice, Pat?

Sure you don't want some champagne ... a brandy ... or maybe a large Cuban cigar?'

If I could have dug a hole in the carpet of the players' lounge and buried myself I'd have done it there and then. The bar manager had told my new boss every single drink I had ordered and even thrown in the cigar for good measure. Howard knew I was embarrassed but said no more, passed me my orange juice and told me not to be late for training on the Monday. What a man-manager he was! He could have bollocked me for getting pissed the night I met him as it was my medical the following day. He could have made a show of me in front of my new team-mates to teach me a lesson, but no, he quietly let me know that wherever I ventured in this huge city, he would no doubt hear about it, hence I learnt that I could not take the piss as I had done in Birmingham.

In training on the Monday, Mr Kendall went on to tell me that Terry Darracott, his chief scout, had watched me about ten times and had noticed I was naturally a right-footed player and had said to Howard that that could be a problem. Howard told me that he'd replied, 'We're having him ... we can work on his left foot ... I like him!'

By Christ, did they work on it! Every day after training, Terry, a tough, hard Scouser, took me out on the pitch and it was left foot this, left foot that and, within a few weeks, I began to find it so much more comfortable not only controlling the ball but crossing and passing with it as well.

Terry himself had been a left-back at Everton and was a bit of a cult hero, although he admitted to me his left foot was worse than mine and that he used to whack it over with the outside of his right at every opportunity. Terry and Howard had noted it as a weakness that we were to improve on and it was simple things like that – working on an obvious weakness – that showed I had moved to a bigger and better club. At Birmingham, nobody had ever said to me that my left foot was a weakness; it was as if it wasn't the best but was good enough for Birmingham. Good enough for them, but nowhere near good enough for Everton. Maybe that attitude was the reason Birmingham were up and down like a whore's knickers every season.

After realising that I had been signed by Mr Kendall to impress on the football pitch and not in the bar, I set about training hard to try and get into the first team, a task that was not going to be easy as Everton, after a shaky start, had strung a couple of wins together and were playing reasonably well.

Despite being fit and raring to go, I was sat in the stands for a few games next to Darracott, who just kept telling me, 'Don't watch the game – stay focussed on how our back four play!' It was hard; if Everton were on the attack, I'd obviously follow the play but would get a dig from Terry and the same instructions: 'Watch the fucking back four!' It did my nut in but, after a couple of games, I began to notice how they went about their business and especially the way the full-backs were always just ahead of the two centre-backs. Things began to click in my head and, in training, it seemed easy to slot in thanks to Terry's expert advice, even though it was blunt and to the point!

46

After one training session, I was chomping at the bit and I got brave and went over to the gaffer for a quiet word. I had it in my head what I was going to say, nice and calm, 'Mr Kendall, I'm really training hard and I would love the opportunity to play in the first team. Do you think I will have to wait much longer to get my chance?'

Well, that's what I had intended to say. As it was, I went over and just blurted out, 'Boss ... I want to fucking play Saturday!' That was it, hours of building myself up and that was the best I could come out with! Howard just smiled and said, 'Patience, son, patience ...' and walked off!

We had a couple of away games in a week and I roomed with Gary Stevens. I was very shy, not used to wearing a suit and going down to the restaurant with the players and the directors for tea, so I used to order my meal with Neville Southall and we'd eat in his room talking nonsense for hours before going to bed. It was superb.

I soon settled into life at Everton; it was one big, happy family and there were no cliques. Everybody trained hard, played hard and, apart from Neville, drank hard together. I was still in a hotel and, as soon as I landed there, I was introduced to a player who had also recently signed called Ian Atkins. Another bloke was hanging about and he came over and shook my hand but I had no idea who he was and, later that night, he phoned my room and asked me if I fancied a night on the town. I almost told him to piss off and then he mentioned that he was meeting a few of my team-mates and the bloke concerned turned out to be Terry Curran, who was also an Everton player. I felt a proper idiot for not knowing who he was, but soon was out and about with him and he was quality company.

Within weeks, we were getting birds back to the rooms and getting pissed but, knowing the amount of spies the gaffer had, I decided that I needed to start behaving, so I got Susan to join me in the hotel and, soon after she arrived, I bought a house around the corner from Sharpy in an area near Southport.

From that day, Graeme watched my back. He looked after me like a brother and always did his very best to make sure I kept out of trouble and, more importantly, away from the women. Sadly, despite his superhuman efforts, there was no man on earth capable of managing that!

5

SWEET DREAMS WITH THE TOFFEES

Everton had only kept one clean sheet in their first eight league games of the 1984/85 season and, although we won 5–4 at Watford, I thought that the gaffer was losing patience with the amount of goals we were leaking. I had played two reserve games and we had kept clean sheets in both of them, which was good, as in the previous three games they had leaked a dozen. I was right about the gaffer losing patience as the following week I made my début at Highbury replacing none other than my new best mate John Bailey.

Although Arsenal beat us 1–0, I did reasonably well but, deep down, with coming back from Highbury pointless, I did not, hand on heart, think I had made the number 3 shirt my own. I was so wrong on that account as, apart from a couple of Cup Winners' Cup ties against some Czechoslovakian outfit when I was ineligible to play and three games I missed through injury and suspension, I was an ever-present for the rest of the season, and what a season it was.

I made my home début against Sheffield United. We were a class apart and it was an easy game that I enjoyed as we gave them a 4–0 thumping. I can't remember much about it, apart from the lads telling me to get used to the 'Z Cars' tune we ran out to as it was part of Everton folklore. I had no idea what they were on about but, after a few games, I was hooked like the rest of them and, to this day, every time I hear that music the hairs stand up on the back of my neck.

After another home win against Aston Villa, we were focussed on the next game which was the Merseyside Derby at Anfield. It was manic. The press were in your face all week and the build-up can only be described as one you would have for a Cup Final. I never realised how much it meant to everyone on Merseyside and especially the local lads in the side. It was hard as a so-called 'outsider' to understand just how massive a deal this was for them. I just got on with training and hoped I would be picked for this game which I thought had better live up to expectations, given the way the people around me were behaving.

What a day it turned out to be. From the minute we got to Anfield, I knew this was for me and that the lads were right to be so up for the occasion. Don't get me wrong – I have and always will give 100 per cent while playing in any game, but this game demanded more. You had to give an extra 10 per cent or you would be left behind.

As we were in the tunnel ready to walk out, I looked around and saw people who were usually as cool as you like looking physically sick, and when we went to go out on to the pitch the Liverpool lads were all slapping the 'This is Anfield' sign, while some of our lot were shouting obscenities at them. So much for the 'Friendly Derby'. I had played at Anfield before and the away fans were lost in the far corner of the Anfield Road End but, as we took to the pitch to the wretched sound of 'You'll Never Walk Alone', all I could hear was 'Come on, you Blues …' echoing around the stadium. How, I don't know, but it seemed that half the ground was full of Evertonians and it made it much easier knowing we had so many fans willing us to victory.

The first half came and went and I was playing down the left flank over to the Kemlyn Road Stand. When I had been there with Birmingham, the abuse you got, albeit quite humorous, was never-ending, but today it was like a home game. I'd go to take a throw in and rows and rows of Evertonians would stand up and applaud – it was superb, I was only chucking the ball back into play!

I thought the second half would be different as I was going to be patrolling the far end near the world-famous Kop and the gaffer told me at half-time to stand tall and not to dive in, as the occupants of that end were quite often responsible for a few dubious penalty awards. I jogged over and kept my head down and it was a fantastic sight when the whole end applauded Neville Southall. Fair play, I thought, as I took my position, but was thinking, 'I wonder if you'll be so gracious if we score?'

It didn't take long to find out and, just a few minutes into the second half, Gary Stevens played a long ball down the centre between Hansen and Lawrenson and Sharpy took a touch before smashing a 25-yard volley over Bruce Grobbelaar's head. The place went bonkers! I was at the wrong end of the pitch to get involved with mobbing him – it wasn't my thing anyway, it was a team game, and I always felt that the goalscorers got a lot of credit that the rest of us also deserved. I noticed a load of fans had run on the pitch and thought it could spell trouble, but it was just Evertonians going mental. I turned to the Kop to see what their reaction was and, I swear to this day, I have seen nothing like it, there must have been 8,000 Evertonians in there jumping up and down. What 'famous' Kop?

Things eventually calmed down and we coped with ease with anything Liverpool threw at us and really should have won by a greater margin. The final whistle saw another pitch invasion as hundreds of Evertonians celebrated our first victory on enemy soil for 14 years and I was pleased, although surprised, that there was not a mass outbreak of violence. I really could not imagine similar scenes at a Villa in a Blues Derby, but that's Merseyside for you, it's a one-off type of place.

In the dressing room, you could still hear the Evertonians singing 'Going down ...' as the Reds had slipped into the bottom three, to a fast-emptying Kop. Well, one half of it was empty, the other half was full of celebrating Blues.

There was talk of us challenging for the title, and rightly so – we were unbeaten in 13 and had just beaten the current champions in their own back yard, but the gaffer kept things in check and his catchphrase of 'one game at a time' was continually drummed into us.

The following Tuesday we flew out to play Inter Bratislava in the Cup Winners' Cup second round and I was gutted to miss out as I had signed after the deadline, meaning that I could not play unless we made it through to the quarter-finals. Obviously, I had been doing OK; the proof was in the results and it helped that we didn't now have to score three or four goals to win games like we had been doing earlier on in the season.

Bails came in for me and I wished him well and he joked that if we kept a clean sheet, the gaffer had told him I'd be back with the reserves and that I'd only been keeping the shirt warm for him while he had a rest and got 100 per cent fit. Joking aside, I was pleased when we did win, but a bit concerned with the clean sheet, as I wondered whether Mr Kendall would think there would be any need to change a winning side that had played well and not conceded. I then began to doubt whether Bails had been joking – had I really been keeping the shirt warm for him?

I had nothing to panic about as, on the Friday after training, Mr Kendall pulled me to one side and told me to get an early night, stay off the beer and that I was back in the side to face United. I swear I could have kissed him; these were exciting times for the club and, after years of playing in a struggling side, I was now in with a chance of actually winning something other than a yard of ale competition or a punch-up in the pub!

United were many people's favourites for the League; Ron Atkinson had put a decent side together and it was arguably the toughest game I was going to be involved in since my move to Goodison. Wrong! It was a stroll in the park. Ladies and gentlemen, I can tell you hand on heart that all I can remember about that game is taking a few throw-ins and free kicks given for offside, not bothering with a shower, getting my suit on and heading straight for the Continental Nightclub!

We absolutely battered United; Sheeds scored with a header and when things like that happen it's like Christmas, your birthday and popping your cherry all at once! It ended up 5–0, and could have been more, but who cares? Yes, gaffer, we will take one game at a time, but bring them on thick and fast! This is what I came here for, but I thought it may take it bit longer than a month before I was in a side playing football of such a superb standard.

A few days later, we travelled to Old Trafford to play United in a League Cup match and we knew it would be tougher; it had to be and it was. We went through 2–1 thanks to a John Gidman own-goal, but a win is a win and we were now unbeaten since my début at Arsenal and, although there was no such thing as an easy game, we had a few coming up that we would fancy our chances in.

The gaffer did his upmost to keep our feet on the ground but we were flying and battered Leicester and Stoke at home, beat West Ham away and eased passed Bratislava

4–0 on aggregate in another game when Bails kept the shirt warm for me! The win against Leicester had seen us go top of the League; things quite simply couldn't have been any better. We had drawn Grimsby at home in the League Cup and went into the game understandably full of confidence; we were simply oozing the stuff, had a settled side and fancied ourselves to progress at the expense of a team a couple of leagues below us. They beat us 1–0!

It was one of the most one-sided games I have ever played in. We simply annihilated them but could not score, so it was unbelievable when they got out of their own box and forced a corner in the last minute and scored from it seconds before the referee blew up for full time. I was expecting some stick from the crowd but they were superb and we were applauded off the pitch. They fully appreciated that we had played well and, in hindsight, I believe that game may have been the one that brought us back down to earth and set us up for the rest of the season.

Things dipped a bit and, in some quarters, people started saying our bubble had burst as we got hammered 4–2 a few days later at Norwich, when at one stage we were 3–0 down and it looked like we could end up being beaten by 5 or 6. We pulled it back to 3–2 before they broke and got a fourth to finish us off and, to make matters worse, I was hauled off by Mr Kendall, although he did reassure me that it was a tactical decision and that I was no worse than any of the others out there – great man-management!

Before that game I met a girl who worked at the hotel reception called Lyn Bentley; we had a chat and got on great but nothing happened as at the time I was on my best behaviour. She sent a letter to Howard Kendall at the club asking him if he'd get me to call her. After assuring the gaffer that I had done nothing the night before the defeat, he agreed that next time we were down there I could have her number.

Sheffield Wednesday came to Goodison the following week and it was a horrible game, with a horrendous tackle from Brian Marwood ending Adrian Heath's season. I was very close to Inchy and was gutted for him, as were all of the lads, and things boiled over when Peter Reid took the law into his own hands and nailed Marwood as Inchy was on his way to hospital. It was confirmed after the game that Adrian was indeed out for the season and it felt in the dressing room that things may just have started to go against us, although the gaffer reassured us that every team would have a 'blip' and that we just needed to keep doing what we had been doing all season and the results would come.

Heath's injury was a massive blow. He had scored 13 goals already that season and the way he played off Graeme Sharp was poetry in motion, but on the bench we had a certain gentleman who liked a challenge, who was up for a scrap and had the knack of scoring the odd goal or two. Andy Gray was a perfect replacement for Inchy and, even though he kept telling anyone who cared to listen what he was going to do, I doubt even Andy could have dreamed up the impact he had on our fortunes for the second half of the season. His presence also had an impact on my appearance total that season and my bank balance as, thanks to him, I missed a couple of games and was fined a week's wages after an incident in our first match together.

We were down at Queen's Park Rangers, who at the time played on a plastic pitch, so it was always going to be difficult for us. I hated those pitches. My game involved a fair bit of tackling and physical contact but on those artificial pitches one sliding tackle could seriously hurt you. Now I don't mind the odd carpet burn, if you get my drift, but even I have a pain threshold!

It was during the second half when it all kicked off as Andy went into a challenge with Simon Stainrod and a bit of a scuffle broke out, so I ran 20 yards to back my man up. Howard Kendall had drummed it into us that on and off the pitch we were to stick together, so in I went. Within seconds, I whacked Stainrod and was then volleyed all over the place by half the QPR team, while Andy Gray stood back and watched. So much for sticking together!

I was sent off and then, as I took the dreaded walk to the dressing rooms, the look the gaffer threw at me made me realise it was one scrap I should have stayed out of. The Everton fans suddenly started chanting, 'Psycho ... Psycho!' Although I appreciated their sentiment, I decided against giving them a wave as I trudged down the tunnel, as I knew Howard was unimpressed with my dismissal.

We held out for a draw and, on the Monday morning, I was summoned to Mr Kendall's office, was fined a week's wages and warned about my future conduct on the pitch. He went on to say that if we were going to win anything, we needed 11 players out there, but I commented that the fine was a bit harsh as he had told us to stick together. He replied, 'We do ... the money will go in the pot for our end-of-season piss-up in Magaluf.' That made it a bit easier to bear.

My main worry was that I would miss two games through suspension which kicked in after our next game at home to Nottingham Forest. I was on my best behaviour as we hammered them 5–0 and sat out the two games over Christmas. We lost the first, 4–3 at home to Chelsea. The defeat was a big blow to our title hopes as the teams above us won and we dropped to third. Spurs went top, United and Liverpool were on our tails and there was hardly a point between us all. Had my moment of madness at QPR ruined our season or, worse still, ruined my chances of trying to make amends?

I thought conceding four at home would maybe work in my favour. I realise that is a selfish way of looking at it and I did not want us to drop points or concede goals but I wanted to be part of the team and play every week. In the players' lounge, everyone was quiet, especially Bails, and I felt for him as he must have been thinking – after waiting so long for a chance to win his place back – collectively the team had cocked it up for him.

We travelled up to Sunderland on Boxing Day and Gary Stevens missed the match though injury. His deputy Alan Harper was also injured, so Ian Atkins came in at right-back. Bailey did really well so I got thinking I may get a game at centre-half, but Mountfield scored both our goals in a 2–1 win so it looked like I was going to struggle to win my place back thanks to that stupid fight with Stainrod. Despite my own selfish thoughts, the mood was great on the way home with everyone happy and we shared a beer or two on the coach. The games were coming thick and fast, though, and we had to travel to Ipswich the following day, so it was a mild Christmas celebration.

I was selected to play at right-back at Portman Road, which was fine by me – as I have said, I'm naturally right-footed. Bails was on the left and we had some great banter throughout the game which we won 2–0. I was shouting over to him, 'Is that shirt a bit tight on you?' He would yell back some obscenity and it was fantastic to play with him but such a pity that we never did so more often, as he was a truly superb professional and, as I've said before, a fantastic person.

Over the holiday period, as well as Bails and Atkins, Terry Curran came in for Andy Gray and we won all three games and were joint top on goal difference with Spurs. It showed that we had a good squad as well as just a starting 11. Alan Harper and Kev Richardson could play anywhere, so it was not just myself sweating on my place when everyone was declared fit for our next match – an awkward cup tie away at Leeds United.

Mr Kendall announced the side on the day of the game: Southall, Stevens, Van Den Hauwe, Ratcliffe, Mountfield, Reid, Steven, Gray, Sharp, Bracewell and Sheedy. He had shown his hand – his first-choice 11 – although he also reminded us of the calibre of players waiting to come in if anyone got complacent or was not doing their job. I was on cloud nine; this was the team that could make history for Everton Football Club and I wanted to be part of it so much it hurt.

A week after the trip to Leeds we played Newcastle off the park at Goodison, beating them 4–0 to go back to the top of the League where we were to remain for the rest of the season. It was an unbelievable run we went on and were unbeaten for 28 games before losing to Forest a few days before our famous trip to Rotterdam. It's never nice getting beaten but, by then, we had already been crowned champions so, although the run came to an end, I can't remember Howard throwing any tea cups at us after the game!

Having got top spot back, we still had almost 20 games to play, but there was a deep belief within the squad that on our day we could beat anybody. Along the way, we had to dig deep at times, none more so than on trips to Leicester and Old Trafford in late February and early March.

I never liked playing at Filbert Street. It was a horrible, run-down shit-hole of a ground, the pitch was poor and I had not had much joy there with Birmingham. Along with Wimbledon and Luton, it was a ground I never enjoyed playing at. It's hard to explain, but I never seemed to get out of the starting block at those places.

In the lead up to the game, the press had been getting on Andy Gray's back, mentioning that since he had replaced Adrian he had not scored. In fairness to Andy, his game was far more than just goals ... just as well really! Joking aside, he had fitted in brilliantly and Sharpy had, according to

Andy, been getting goal after goal on the back of his assists and hard work. Strikers, however, lived and died by their goal per game ratio and, as it stood, Andy's was none in ten, and even John Bailey knew that was not great and he was piss-poor at maths!

That changed at Leicester and Gray scored a brace, a cracking half-volley to win us the game and a trademark header when he put his nut where very few others would dare to go! Up front for Leicester was a young Gary Lineker, and it took the brilliance of Neville in goal to secure our win and to stop Lineker getting a hatful. I think that day Howard decided that Lineker's pace could cause any defence problems and noted it in his little black book.

A draw at Old Trafford was a good point earned despite the fact that we missed a late penalty. Four days later, I made my European début in a 3–0 win against the Dutch outfit Fortuna Sittard when Andy Gray notched a hat-trick to give us an outstanding chance of making the semi-finals.

Another draw at Villa when we played really poorly gave Spurs a chance to overtake us at the top but they did not take it and when we beat Arsenal at home and Southampton away, our visit to White Hart Lane was regarded by some sections of the media as a 'title decider'. What a game that was.

Gray scored early on; then Trevor Stevens went through and rounded the 'keeper to send the Everton masses into ecstasy. But one of their defenders thumped a pile-driver in with a few minutes to go, to set up a finale that was more like the Alamo. With the last attack of the game, they won a corner and it was met by their big forward Falco who beat us to the ball and thundered a header in. I never even bothered to look and stood there thinking our lack of concentration had cost us dearly.

As I turned round for the inevitable inquest as to whose fault it was, the lads were mobbing Southall, congratulating him on one of his greatest ever saves. Somehow, he had managed to tip Falco's bullet header from point-blank range over the bar and that was the very moment I knew we were going to be crowned champions sooner rather than later.

Back in the dressing room, we were ecstatic, apart from Nev, who sat there with his customary cup of tea bemoaning the fact that he had been beaten from 20 yards and had not managed to hold Falco's header! Southall was a perfectionist; he could keep a clean sheet and get the man of the match award after saving a couple of penalties, but he would still pick holes in his own performance. The man was destined to become one of the world's greatest ever goalkeepers, which indeed he did.

I missed the next game at home to Sunderland when we won 4–1 having gone a goal down in the first few minutes. Poor old Bails must have thought he was our unlucky charm but, once again, Andy Gray came up trumps with a couple of classic headers as we coasted to victory. Unlike previous games I had missed, I was comfortable that I would be back given Mr Kendall's previous call that his strongest 11 contained my good self.

As well as the league games, we were slowly getting on with our job in Europe. Everton had never won a European trophy and were probably the biggest British club not to have done so. It was a tough ask, though, as we were paired with cup favourites Bayern Munich after we saw off Sittard 2–0 in the away leg.

My memory is not the best concerning individual games, but I will never forget a streaker running on the pitch in Sittard. To our dismay, though, it was a bloke – and to piss us off further he was a 'big' bloke, if you see where I'm coming from! Now I am not one for running around after these publicity-seeking idiots, and this bloke was on the opposite side of the pitch anyway, so I watched as he pranced about a bit before trying to climb over the fence to rejoin the crowd. He was lucky as, just as he was scaling the fence, a police dog handler appeared with this huge Rottweiler that had his eye on the bloke's sausage and, to this day, I don't know if the poor fella was ever able to have kids despite his couple of minutes of fame!

The trip to Bayern was always going to be tough but, to make matters worse, we had a few injuries and both Andy Gray and Kevin Sheedy missed out. Mr Kendall showed his class as a manager and played five across the middle to contain the Germans and we dug deep. Although it was hard at times, we held out for a goalless draw, a truly great result. It was during games like that when we realised how important the likes of Alan Harper and Kevin Richardson were to us; no matter when or where they were asked to play, they came in and never let us down, fantastic lads and model professionals. No matter who in the squad came in as cover, we were like a well-oiled machine and the result was poetry in motion.

The game in Munich was one of the hardest games I ever played in; those Germans could run all day, were disciplined and were also very good footballers with the likes of Augenthaler, Matthäus, Hoeness and Rummenigge as household names. I'm not sure if they had heard of Van Den Hauwe, Sharp, Ratcliffe or even Andy Gray, but I'll tell you what – by the time we had finished with them, they wished they hadn't!

To get them back to Goodison on level terms made us favourites and that's all the gaffer had asked us to do. We never went out looking for a draw, but he drummed it into us that if we could get them at our place needing to win by a single goal, he'd be happy. Happy he was!

A lot has been said about the home game with Bayern. I still stand by what I've said about it – to this day, it stands as the best game of my life, it was quite simply as good as it gets. The atmosphere that night will never be bettered. We went on to win cups and, although we never actually won anything that night apart for a game of football, that night, believe me, was the night to end all nights.

We showed our character and the quality we also had in our side to come back from a goal down and beat them 3–1. They were bit upset about the way we got stuck into them in the second half but there is no other way I can put this – fuck them! We had not gone that far to be rolled over by a bunch of Germans playing pretty football. We had to match them in every department and that's what we did and the noise that greeted our goals and the final whistle was something I think about all the time. As I have said, nothing has ever matched it since.

After that game, we let our hair down a bit, but we were a couple of wins away from clinching the title, so it was nothing too crazy … honest! I seriously had to pinch myself to make sure this was all real – for years, I'd been playing in a struggling team with no hope of winning anything. Now I was a few games away from clinching the treble. I was in dreamland, and it was a feeling I never wanted to end!

By the weekend we had recovered, had plenty of rest and knew if we beat Norwich then the League Championship was almost ours. We breezed it and hammered them 3–0. Our strikers drew blanks but, as usual, others weighed in with the goals and the usual suspects, Mountfield and Steven, were joined on the score sheet by Paul Bracewell.

At times like this, there is a danger that nerves can get to you, but we were so confident in our own and each other's ability that we knew if we did things that came naturally to us then we would win, it really was as simple as that. Howard, Colin Harvey and Mick Heaton were superb and kept us in line, never letting us get carried away but, at the same time, installing a will to win and inner strength into us that made us confident without being blasé. Those three men were fantastic at their jobs.

We went to Sheffield Wednesday a week later and, although it was not one of our better performances, we ground out a 1–0 win. It was another clean sheet for Neville but how he kept one that day only he will know. People mention the save at Spurs, but that day he pulled off a couple that I was close to and, I kid you not, they were out of this world. One save – I think it was from Varadi – was unbelievable and, as he walked past me shaking his head, he muttered, 'I fucking give up!' Neville must have been a forward's worst nightmare. Like Varadi that day, they often did everything right, but were still unable to beat our big man between the sticks.

From being neck and neck with Spurs just a few weeks earlier, we were now 11 points clear and clinched the league two days after the win at Sheffield on a bank holiday Monday against QPR. Unlike our last meeting, there was no way this lot were going to spoil my day. Before the game, Howard gave us all the usual script: 'Go out and do your jobs and the game will be won ...' adding, '... and we will be champions!' Every single one of us went down that tunnel knowing we would not let him down; we never did and I was happy to sling a cross over with my left foot late on that Sharpy headed in to seal a 2–0 victory and to get Goodison rocking.

It was a bit of a let-down that some prick in a suit at the FA had decided that we could not get the trophy that day, although we were eventually presented with it two days later after beating West Ham 3–0. We had played three games in five days, used just 12 players, scored 6 and conceded 0 and not moaned once about being tired or needing squad rotation ... and I loved every minute of it!

The following week, our unbeaten run came to an end

with a defeat at Forest. After the game, we saw the scenes at Bradford on TV where 56 spectators died and more than 200 were injured as a fire ripped through the Main Stand at Valley Parade during a game with Lincoln City. I had never seen anything like it, it was horrific, and I'm just glad that the tragedy was seen by many as a wake-up call for English clubs to improve the state of their grounds. That disaster could have happened at any ground in the country, including our own. On the same day at Birmingham, my ex-team-mates clinched promotion but a young boy was killed when a wall collapsed on him during a disturbance outside St Andrew's. Losing our unbeaten run meant nothing on such a tragic day for football.

With one cup in the Goodison cabinet, we still had another two to go for, so off we went to Rotterdam to face Rapid Vienna. Things were moving so fast for me I never had time to think about how important these games were. We landed in Holland, had a look around the ground, did a few stretches and slept. There was no need to train as such, as we were super fit with the amount of games we were playing.

The worry about the Vienna game was that everyone knew they were no Bayern Munich. Of course, they were a good side, they had made it to the final, but we knew we were better than them. It took a few words from the gaffer and coaches, not so much to tell us about being too cocky, but more of a warning that we had come so far, so don't fuck it up now!

The night went totally to plan and we were cruising with

a couple of minutes to go and, despite them getting a late goal to pull it back to 2–1, we went up the other end, Sheeds made it 3–1 and Everton's first European trophy was bagged. Going up the steps to get my medal was like a fairytale … I could not get my nut round it!

In just eight months I had left a struggling side and was now on the verge of winning the treble. Although we sadly missed out on that, it was the most amazing time of my life. It was so good that even in my darkest hours the memories kept me in good spirits. I am so proud to have been a member of that team and played my part in making it such a fantastic season for Everton Football Club.

As a child, when you are kicking a ball about with your mates in the street or in the school playground you dream of playing in front of thousands of people and the pinnacle of that dream is holding a cup above your head as those thousands of people chant your name.

That season, my dream came true.

6

ENGLAND
EXPECTS ...

With playing in such a successful side as Everton, winning cups and getting rave reviews from quite a few so-called 'experts', I suppose it was only a matter of time before I was approached to play for my country. But even by my own unpredictable standards, it did shock me when it was a Welsh shirt I pulled on for my international début!

Everton had played Manchester United on the Saturday and I was called in by the gaffer who told me that the Belgium manager Guy Thiess had been at the match. He'd wanted to have a look at me and have a chat to see if I was interested in being selected for my country of birth. It was a no-brainer – of course I was. Most of the lads were away during international breaks and, although I did not mind playing head tennis and five-a-side with the kids, I was a bit pissed off at having no drinking partners to go out with.

Remember, at that time Southall and Ratcliffe were Welsh regulars; Gary Stevens, Trevor Steven, Reidy and Paul Bracewell had all made the England squad; Andy Gray and Sharpy were with Scotland; even Sheeds had landed himself in the Irish squad, leaving myself, Bails, Derek Mountfield, Inchy (who was mostly on the treatment table) and the super-subs Kev Richardson and Alan Harper as the only senior players turning up at Bellfield during the week.

About an hour later, Guy called and immediately I was not impressed. He harped on about the style of play he liked his teams to play and told me I would have to adapt if I was to make the grade as I had so much to learn. I thought he was on the blower to try and persuade me to join his side – which, by the way, were not really up there with the Brazils and Italys of world football – not to give me a lecture about how shit I was! Things got worse when he kept telling me about how Enzo Scifo pulled all the strings on the pitch, and when I remarked that I had never heard of him, I swear I thought he had fainted because the line went silent.

Eventually, he offered me a chance to play for the Under-21s as an over-age player to see if I could 'adapt' to this world-beating system he had bored the arse off me with for the last 20 minutes. I told him I would consider his offer and put the phone down.

Despite thinking the bloke was a bit of a clown, I still was realistic enough to know that I'd have to consider his crap offer if I was to fulfil all footballers' dreams of playing in a major tournament like the World Cup finals. Howard asked me how things had gone and he could sense that I was not too thrilled by Guy's plans for me, and he told me to wait a day or two as a couple of other managers wanted a chat with me and that England had been on to him asking if I'd make contact.

Now, I had a British passport as I had been in England since the age of five, and my mother was born in London, so obviously I thought that I could play for England. I was excited about what Howard had told me, so I got the number and my call was answered by England – Mike England, manager of Wales! I'd been expecting to be put through to Bobby Robson, manager of England!

I hit it off with Mike at once – he was fantastic. He told me that Big Nev and Rats had told him I was doing a great job for Everton and that Ian Rush had also put a word in for me and that if I was interested then I could meet up with the squad for the next game with the view of getting my international career off the ground. I was highly impressed with the way he went about selling the job to me and found him to be a very honest and genuine bloke. Everything I found out about him since has confirmed this initial impression, and I still think the same way about him to this day.

My mind was made up and I decided that it was a far better bet to play for Wales than to play for Belgium. Now, if I am 100 per cent honest, I will admit this was not purely a football decision, as I was informed by a journalist that if I opted to play for my country of birth then I may have had to do nine months' national service in the Belgian Army!

Wales were a decent side but were lacking strength in depth; as well as the Everton duo they had Rushy, who, at the time, was world class, Mark Hughes was making a name for himself and the likes of Joey Jones and Mickey Thomas were seasoned campaigners, even though they were probably on the wrong side of their careers. I thought Wales were probably just a few players away from being a really good side who could match Europe's élite. If I could help, I was bang up for it as it seemed a far better bet than playing for Guy Thiess and his amazing formation led by Mr Scifo. It was also hard to forget that there was a chance I'd be square bashing, polishing boots and belt buckles as well as shooting bullets out of World War II rifles at tin cans all week.

The following day, just as my mind was made up and I was about to tell Mr England my decision, I got a call from Bobby Robson asking me if I'd consider joining up with the England lads for a get-together with a view to playing in a forthcoming friendly.

My head was battered, I was in absolute pieces and was glad that Howard, as always, was there to offer his expert advice. Basically, he told me to take my time and again weigh up all the options. He had been a quality player – part of Everton's legendry midfield who, along with Colin Harvey and the late great Alan Ball, were etched in Goodison folklore as 'The Holy Trinity'. However, he had missed out on an international career having played at all levels for England apart from the full squad, which to this day many people find hard to believe given the talent he had.

Quite simply, he told me to see who may get a game before me, so I looked at what England had and it was a scary line-up of players who I'd have to shift if I was to get a cap or two. Alan Kennedy was a great left-back but had won just a couple of caps given that Kenny Sansom was first choice. I asked myself if I could get in before those two, let alone a handful of others who, like myself, were on the fringes of being called up. Howard then told me that he had recommended me to both Mr England and Mr Robson as a centre-half, which I truly appreciated as it showed the kind of faith he had in my ability.

Obviously, I contacted my parents and told them the difficult situation I had found myself in and it made matters worse when my father told me I should play for Belgium and my mother told me I had to choose England ... so, being an awkward bugger, I opted for Wales!

Joking aside, my reasoning was that although Wales were not really in with the same chance as England to qualify for the World Cup finals, I would stick to my original decision and join up with the Wales squad.

Within the time it took me to decide between England and Wales, a bit of friction had surfaced between the two managers, with Mike accusing Bobby of unsettling me and trying to scupper his chances of me playing for him, even though Bobby never really intended to select me for England. Although it was nice to be wanted, I was a little upset by it all as, despite what people think about me, I am quite a shy person and found the fuss a little embarrassing. During this time, may I add that Guy Thiess had made no attempt to try and make me turn down both the home countries in favour of Belgium. And no one from the Belgian Army had been desperate for my services either!

I called Mike and we agreed that I would join the next squad and looked forward to becoming an international footballer. Little did I know at the time that it was a decision which nearly ended my professional career a couple of years later, but more of that later.

There was quite a bit of a reaction in the press about my choice of nations, with some people questioning my right to play for a country that I had no ties with. Kevin Ratcliffe was supportive and mentioned in the press that I was more than welcome to play for Wales, while Mike England was quoted as saying, 'It is my job to select the best team available from the players available, and that is what I have done.'

I will make it quite clear that, despite some articles claiming I had Welsh blood in me, I did not. No parent or grandparent – or even great-grandparents – of mine were Welsh. In fact, apart from an uncle from South London who claimed he had been sent to Rhyl as a child during the War, no members of my immediate family had even set foot on Welsh soil.

Undeterred, I set off with Neville and Rats and joined up with my new 'international' team-mates prior to a World Cup qualifier against Spain at Wrexham's Racecourse

Above: One of my first ever tackles playing for Arsenal Juniors!

Below: Back row, second left, one of the odd days I was in school.

Welcome Pat!

Pat Van den Hauwe, the 23-year-old Birmingham City left-back, signed for Everton on Friday 21st September. Born in Belgium but brought up in London, he joined Birmingham as an apprentice in 1977 and made 123 League appearances, the last 59 consecutively. Pat will be featured in the magazine for one of next week's matches.

Above: Joining Birmingham City with Mark Dennis.

Below left: Welcome! My introduction in the Everton programme.

Below right: With Susan, Mrs Van Den Hauwe 'No1' shortly after my move to Goodison.

Above: Taff Van Den Hauwe! My Welsh debut with Everton team mates Big Nev and Kevin Ratcliffe.

Below: Mike England's Welsh squad.

Above: Dreams come true, League Champions 1984–85.

Below: Rotterdam 1985, Oh what a night!

Inset: Job Done! One the return flight home from Rotterdam with the CWC .

Above: Norman Whiteside ruins our dream of The Treble.

Below: 'Business as usual!' The Goal That Won the Title!

Right: Psycho Chiller! Sort out Psycho. Bad press was never too far away when I played!

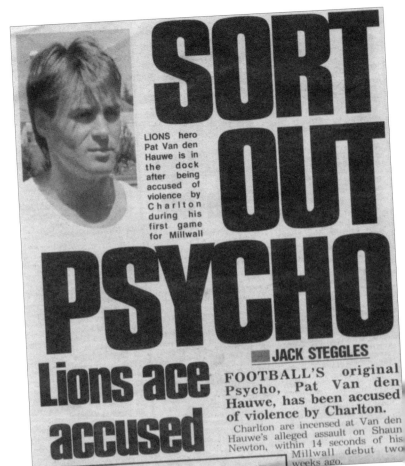

LIONS hero Pat Van den Hauwe is in the dock after being accused of violence by Charlton during his first game for Millwall

SORT OUT PSYCHO

Lions ace accused

■ JACK STEGGLES

FOOTBALL'S original Psycho, Pat Van den Hauwe, has been accused of violence by Charlton.

Charlton are incensed at Van den Hauwe's alleged assault on Shaun Newton, within 14 seconds of his Millwall debut two weeks ago.

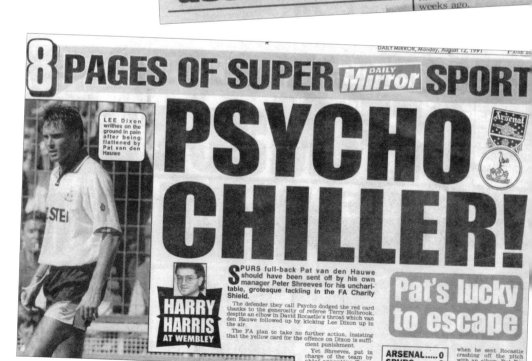

DAILY MIRROR, Monday, August 12, 1991   PAGE 28

8 PAGES OF SUPER *Daily Mirror* SPORT

LEE DIXON writhes on the ground in pain after being flattened by Pat van den Hauwe

PSYCHO CHILLER!

Pat's lucky to escape

HARRY HARRIS AT WEMBLEY

SPURS full-back Pat van den Hauwe should have been sent off by his own manager Peter Shreeves for his uncharitable, grotesque tackling in the FA Charity Shield.

The defender they call Psycho dodged the red card thanks to the generosity of referee Terry Holbrook, despite an elbow in David Rocastle's throat which van den Hauwe followed up by kicking Lee Dixon up in the air.

The FA plan to take no further action, insisting that the yellow card for the offence on Dixon is sufficient punishment.

Yet Shreeves, put in charge of the team by chief executive Terry Venables, admirably

| ARSENAL | 0 |
| SPURS | 0 |

when he sent Rocastle crashing off the pitch with an elbow. But Rocastle holds no grudges despite his anger

Above: A battle with Mick Harford. A real 'Hardman'.

Left: Mersey Man!

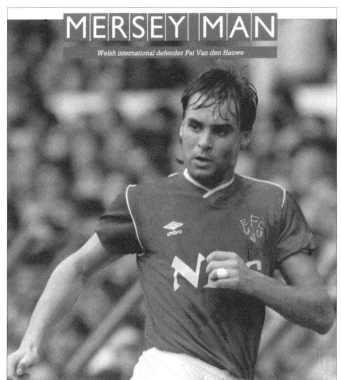

MERSEY MAN

Welsh international defender Pat Van den Hauwe

Oh Mandy! Leaving the register office. If only I had not said 'I do!'

Ground, so my hope of world travel began with a 15-mile car journey.

I had the début that dreams are made of. Spain were a decent side and had battered Wales in a group game six months earlier but, with a full house of about 25,000 roaring us on, we annihilated them 3–0. Ian Rush got a couple and Mark Hughes scored what I believe was voted goal of the season to send the locals home very happy indeed. The goal from Sparky was typical of him – the ball came in at a height that 99 per cent of forwards would have got their head to, but Mark dipped his shoulder and fired an unstoppable scissor-kick into the top corner. Very few players would have been able to execute that shot perfectly, but to him it was common practice.

Before this game, it was mentioned that Wales had four world-class players in Southall, Ratcliffe, Hughes and Rush; after the game, Mike England had been so impressed with my performance he told that I had joined the others and nicknamed me 'Dai Five'!

Despite the dream start, even after one game I had doubts about how far the team could go as although we now had five players whom the gaffer deemed as international class, the remainder of the side was made from clubs such as Bristol Rovers, Watford and Oxford. I am not trying in any way to be disrespectful to the lads at these clubs, but the facts are that half the team were unheard of outside their own back yard and we were supposed to be competing with Europe's finest.

However, what we lacked in quality and strength in depth

was offset by the way the lads stuck together and went about their business and, from day one, it was evident that the team spirit was second to none. With Mike England in charge, we were always in with a chance of causing an upset or two as the Spaniards had just found out.

My next game was typical of the luck – or lack of it – that Wales had over the years. We needed to beat Scotland to make the World Cup play-offs and the game had a bit of extra spice for the Everton lads as Graeme Sharp and Andy Gray were playing for the Jocks. There was no softly-softly approach to these pair of buggers; it was business as usual and myself and Kevin agreed to give the pair of them a few knocks early on to let them know this was international football, not a club friendly at Bellfield. The problem was they obviously felt the same and, from the first minute, they were at it, leaving an arm in here and an elbow in there, usually in my ear, in Andy's case.

The game at Ninian Park was a full house with loads of Scots in the near 40,000 crowd and it started well when we went one up after an early Mark Hughes goal. It was no classic with so much at stake, and they were not causing us too many problems when the ref gave them a penalty late on for a nothing handball. Davie Cooper kept his cool and slotted the ball past Big Nev; they saw the game out and, once again, Wales had fallen at the final hurdle.

I was really pissed off. I was close to the penalty incident and, to this day, feel the referee cheated us, harsh words that would probably get me in big trouble in this day and age. But it was 25 years ago, so bollocks to it – we were cheated out of the chance of playing in the greatest tournament in football.

After the game, the news reached the dressing room that Scotland's manager Jock Stein had been taken ill and had sadly died. That was tragic and it put things into perspective. The referee was fortunate, as the headlines were rightly focused on Mr Stein's passing, and not the scandalous decision he had made.

I went out after the game to drown my sorrows and ended up bringing a local girl back to the hotel. I managed to sneak her into the health suite and we set about having a good time. We were in the middle of doing what comes naturally in the sauna when a security guard came in and politely told me to pack it in and asked her to leave. It was a bad night all round.

A few days later I got a call from one of the girls at Everton who worked on the switchboard asking me to call a young lady who had left her number. I was never one to pass on the chance of a potential kiss and cuddle, so called the number to be greeted by this demented cow from the sauna accusing me of stealing her watch! I politely told her that I would not do such a thing as I earned enough money to buy a box of watches, but she kept on and threatened to sell the story of our hotel romp and the alleged watch theft to the papers. I called her bluff and told her to go ahead and put the phone down, although I must admit that for a week or two I read the papers to see if she had carried out her threat.

Despite the disappointment of missing out on the World

Cup finals, I was fully committed to my international career and was looking forward to giving it my best shot when the European Championships began the following season. Mr England had rightly been given a vote of confidence from the Welsh FA, who, so far, I had not had the privilege of meeting. All the players were up for the challenge ahead, although the next game gave me an inkling that the Welsh public saw things slightly differently.

I was called up for a friendly against Hungary at Cardiff and it was a nightmare, a cold miserable October night and just over 3,000 turned up to watch us get hammered 3–0. I hated playing in front of such crap crowds as, when the fans abuse you, not only can you hear what they are shouting at you, you can spot the individual calling you all sorts. That night they were calling me a few things I had not been called before and, may I add, they were not speaking Welsh.

Next up was a friendly in Saudi Arabia which I pulled out of and, in all honesty, I can understand why some of today's top players go missing for such games. The club never put me under any pressure to miss any Wales games, but our brief on international friendlies was always, 'If you are not 100 per cent fit, don't play …' So if I had the odd niggle and it was a nothing game, I would do as I was told and made the call, simple as! It's worth remembering that I was playing 50-odd games a season, so there was no need to risk potential injury for the sake of making trip halfway across the world that had probably been arranged to give the suits in Cardiff a free holiday anyway.

Nev Southall was the complete opposite – he would turn

out as an over-age player for the Welsh schoolboys if asked. He was totally committed to anything they asked him to do, but this came back to bite him on the arse when he broke his ankle in the next friendly in Ireland when the Lansdowne Road pitch was like a bomb site. As I have said previously, I believe that injury cost Everton big time and it was a pointless game, so make your own mind up about such games. I did, hence my low cap count.

It was at this time when I began to notice that our away friendlies were all in quite exotic places, so fair play to the Welsh FA for sorting them, whatever the reason! As I said, though, I was happy to stay at home and rest and let them get on with it from time to time, so I also missed the following trip to Canada along with the injured Nev, Rats and Rushy, which caused a bit of bad press over there as Wales had promised to bring a full squad as part of the deal. We had just finished a long, hard season and it was days after the first Merseyside Cup Final and we hardly needed to play any more football, so when the FA called to ask me to reconsider to save their arses, by a strange coincidence I was out when the phone rang.

In fairness, the Welsh FA had some decent people on board; they were very proud, patriotic people but with every one good member came two free-loading hangers-on. I used to have a drink and chat with a gentleman called Elfed Ellis, a North Wales Evertonian who was a close friend of Mike England's. He was a true ambassador for the country he loved and enjoyed a drink.

One morning after a game, I thought he was up early

having breakfast before being told by the waitress that he had not been to bed! He would for ever be bringing fans into the hotel and buying them drinks and giving them tickets and his catchphrase to his fellow FA members was: 'These people have put us in this privileged position, so look after them.' It was a shame some of the others never had that attitude; if they had, Wales may have attracted bigger crowds.

The thing I noticed about Wales compared to Everton was that everything seemed to be done on the cheap – the hotels, the travel, the kit, it was all second-rate. Quite often you would see the likes of Kevin Ratcliffe and Ian Rush, world-class players, humping the kit bag at the airport while about 20 FA members made it through to the first-class lounge to hammer the free bar. That kind of thing seriously pissed us off, if the truth be known.

Once again, I was injured along with Nev when we opened our Euro '88 campaign in Helsinki with a 1–1 draw, but we were both back when we drew with Russia in a friendly that I used to improve my match fitness. I also played when we walloped the Finns 4–0 in the return at Wrexham before a dreadful crowd of less than 8,000. We were doing well and I could not get my nut around the fact that we were getting such piss-poor crowds; where had the 30,000 gone from the Scotland game? To make matters worse, I limped off early as my injury nightmare continued.

The next two games were hardly classics but we got a point at home to Czechoslovakia thanks to a late Ian Rush goal, and then gave ourselves a great chance of qualifying when we beat Denmark in Cardiff courtesy of an early Mark Hughes strike. However, once again we contrived to balls it up when we lost the return to the Danes 1–0 in a game we should have got something out of.

I will never forget the few minutes before the kick-off that night. As we were lining up for the national anthems, we stood in line and the Danish tannoy blasted out 'God Save the Queen'! Now, I have nothing against Her Majesty, I am sure she is a very lovely lady, but that was taking the piss and it did not go down well with some of the lads. I never knew the words of our own anthem but, from the first time I heard it, it gave me goose bumps and made the hairs stand up on the back of my neck in the same way the 'Z Cars' theme tune did at Goodison. I was not alone, as very few of the lads sang it, but when it came to the chorus it was stunning, so to hear the wrong one being played before such an important game was not really inspiring.

The defeat meant we had to win in Czechoslovakia to stand any chance of qualifying and we lost 2–0 meaning that, once again, Wales had missed out on going to a major tournament, which was bad for the players but worse for the FA members as they would have to pay for their own summer holidays!

The saddest part of failing to qualify was that Mike England parted company with us and I was very sad to see him go. Mike had given me the chance to play international football and put his head on the block with some people who were against non-Welsh nationals being selected. He had shown great faith in me and I will for ever be thankful to him for that. He was a man's manager and treated people with respect, unlike the bloke appointed to take over from him. Mike's record as manager was decent, with about a 50 per cent win rate, which was excellent considering the limited number of players he had to choose from.

Dave Williams stood in as caretaker boss for a game at Swansea and the public voted with their feet as less than 6,000 turned up to see us get turned over. Our scorer that day was Dean Saunders, a young, confident lad who would play many more times for Wales than myself. This was very frustrating with Wales as it always seemed that as we lost players other good lads came through – the likes of Barry Horne, Gary Speed and Ryan Giggs would be called up, but it was almost always when someone like Joey or Mickey retired. So it was a case of one in, one out, and so we never had a dozen top-class players to take us through to the next level.

Dave must have upset some of the clowns at the Welsh FA HQ with his tactics or probably he was daft enough to send a petrol receipt in, as he was bombed after just one game. I was told that our new gaffer was going to be Terry Yorath, a quite well-respected gentleman who'd had a very creditable playing career. That was all well and good, but as a person I thought within a minute of meeting him that he was an arrogant bully and a total prick.

As I was introduced to him, he grabbed my hand and slapped me across the back of the head with his other hand. It was not a playful pat but a proper slap, and I pulled away from him and said, 'Don't ever fucking do that to me again!'

So after two minutes it was safe to say my Wales career was coming to an end.

Under Yorath I missed a friendly in Sweden, a country I would liked to have visited for all the wrong reasons but agreed to go on an end-of-season 'jolly' as, once again, the FA had come up trumps and sorted us two games in Malta and Italy. I'll once again be bluntly honest and tell you I was going for anything but the football. I had just finished probably my worst season at Goodison during which, although we were always top four, we were never really in a position to challenge for the title, so I thought a few days in the sun would give me a lift and was more than happy to join up with the lads. This was the decision that came close to ending my career, as well as my marriage.

I had ended the season with a slight hamstring niggle, so I sat out the Malta game. However, the night before, knowing I wouldn't be playing, I'd sneaked out to sample the local hospitality, meeting up with a local lady who, shall we say, was quite happy to show me some Maltese delights! I had a stunning night in her company and, the following day, watched the game in between some sunbathing and swimming. My hamstring was improving and, as I sat on the pool side with a beer in my hand and the sun on my back, I thought to myself how could things possibly be any better? Little did I know that inside my body was beginnings of a virus that could hardly be any worse.

We travelled to Italy the following day and I noticed that my ankle had swollen slightly but thought it may have been from the flying or possibly all the swimming I had been doing. The Welsh medical assistant – although he was probably a vet knowing how the Welsh FA liked to save money – strapped me up and I played the full game in Brescia, albeit with some discomfort. We won 1–0 and that night we all went out for a few beers and a meal and, as it happened, I once again ended up with a local lady, so went home in good spirits.

A day or two after arriving home, I began to feel a little discomfort in my nether regions – and I don't mean my ankle – so I went to the club doctor at Everton and, within days, was in hospital and never kicked a ball again for three months. Everton were not happy as, thanks to an Irish pitch and a Maltese bitch, they had lost two of their top players while on international duty, although in slightly different circumstances.

A month later, the club secretary at Everton handed me a letter from Italy and I opened it to discover that it had a medical card stapled to it and, although I can't read Italian, I knew it was from the girl I had slept with in Brescia. I had a good idea what it was about and I was quite sure it was not a request for me to pop back to Italy to marry her.

I was struggling to get fit – injuries are one thing but a blood disorder like mine was extremely hard to get rid of and I was playing a few games then missing a few as I was quite simply not well enough to play regular, top-flight football. I missed the first World Cup qualifier in Holland when the lads played well but got pipped 1–0, but was back in action for a disappointing 2–2 draw at home to Finland. We then had another worthless friendly in Israel that I missed, but I played what turned out to be my last game for Wales on Wednesday, 26 April 1989, just a week or so after the Hillsborough disaster.

The next game was a massive one for Wales, at home to Germany, a game that was to be played at the National Stadium which was usually only used for rugby matches. It was a game any footballer would love to play in, and I was really looking forward to the occasion. Disaster struck during extra time in the Cup Final against Liverpool as, once again, I felt my hamstring go and, after the game, our physio said I'd have to give it a couple of weeks' rest. Then the powers that be phoned the Welsh FA and informed them I was withdrawing from the squad.

The day after the game, I got a call from Yorath and, before I had chance to say hello, he was ranting and raving, accusing me of all sorts and ordered me to get to Cardiff to be assessed by the Welsh medical team.

Now people who know me well will appreciate that I don't take kindly to being ordered about, so basically I told him to fuck off, and he replied that I would never play for Wales again. It was probably not the cleverest thing I have ever said, but on the back of a Cup Final defeat against your bitterest rivals and carrying yet another injury which had plagued me all season, I was in no mood for pleasantries.

These things happen in football and I was expecting Yorath to call me back and get things sorted, but what happened next shocked me as he got on to the press and was quoted the following day calling me a disgrace and saying that my international career was over. Although I took it on the chin, I was bitter about the way Yorath had treated me.

Wales failed to make it to the 1990 World Cup finals in Italy, and I'll be honest and say I was a little mixed up watching Belgium do so well before eventually going out to England when David Platt scored in the last minute of extra time. Had I waited, maybe I would have played in that game for either side – who knows what might have happened? But to this day, I am extremely proud to have played for Wales and, in particular, that great manager and superb person Mike England.

7

HEART WITH A MERSEY BEAT

Liverpool can be a tough, rough place. Make no bones about it, it is a city that has more than its fair share of hard-cases and is certainly a place where the locals do not suffer fools. When I moved to Everton, I was warned by a few people that I may find it hard to get out and enjoy myself as I had a bad reputation which might have been a tag the Scousers wanted to test. And I had another distinct disadvantage ... I was a Londoner!

The people who were worried about my general wellbeing did not know that I had connections in the city – very good connections indeed. Many years before I moved to Goodison, a gentleman named John Smith, who was a well-known local businessman, used to travel to London with the Golden Gloves Boxing Club from Liverpool and fight my local club, the Fisher Amateur Boxing Club. The Fisher lads were trained by Little Nobby, a well-known ex-member of the Krays' firm. Through the boxing, John became friends with my Uncles Harry and Tommy who, at the time, ran The Crown, a well-respected pub in Jamaica Road, Bermondsey.

The Crown was near The Lilliput Pub, run by a Scouse boxer – Billy Aird – who fought for European and British Championships. He had been one of the Golden Glove boxers but liked London so much he decided to stay there. Another boxer who fought the Fisher lads was none other than Wayne Rooney Snr, father of the famous ex-Evertonian who, in his younger days, I'm told, was a decent fighter.

As soon as I moved to Everton, I got in touch with John and, to this day, he remains one of my closest friends, although he has had to clip my wings once or twice since we met. My first introduction to some of his infamous, hands-on discipline came soon after I made the move to Merseyside. I was guilty of turning up at another well-known boxing club, the Everton Red Triangle, pissed up, and foolishly threw John's name into the hat when I was asked to fuck off, having made a bit of a nuisance of myself.

The bloke in charge, Joe Curran, phoned John to say I was acting a bit out of order, so John told him to stick me in the ring with someone while he came down to take me home. I went to the ring upstairs and was put in with a local lad called Tony Carroll and, not realising he was an up-and-coming pro, gladly agreed to spar with him. By the time

John arrived, Tony had literally chased me round the ring, so I got out and told John to join me for a few minutes as this bloke was a bit too tasty for me. It was a big mistake!

John stripped to his vest and asked for these huge 16oz gloves which, when worn, made his hands look like fucking shovels. With not wanting to lose face, I commented that we would just have a bit of a spar and no proper hitting in the face. Tony said he'd keep time and we'd just have a minute, so I got ready. The bell went and 'BOOM', this 16oz glove smashed into my belly and it was game over in two seconds flat. I never turned up pissed at that gym again.

Having learnt a valuable lesson, I began showing a bit more respect and John introduced me to a good friend of his – Tony Unghi. Tony was another well-known local businessman who owned The Royal George in Park Road, Toxteth. I had some fantastic times in that boozer; if ever I had problems or wanted to get away from all the hassle of being in the spotlight, that was the place to go. It was nicknamed 'Black George's' and I was treated like a local in there at all times. When I went missing from training, that's where I would be; it was the one place the likes of Terry Darracott and his staff would not come looking for me. I remember one night shagging a cleaner on the pool table and, from that day on, she was nicknamed Nora Van Den Hauwe by all the punters!

Another great pub John took me to was run by ex-Everton winger Gary Jones called The Albert in Lark Lane. It was another place I spent time in when I should have been elsewhere ... but that's another story. Gary was a fantastic bloke and I was lucky to be over in the UK when he got married and I attended the ceremony with John and his wife Lynne.

I went out quite often with a bloke called Dave Dolby who was also a good friend of Graeme Sharp. Dave, an ex-copper, ran a boozer near where we lived called The Royal Blundell. One day, he sorted it for me to go to the police station, showed me around and we ended up going into the shooting range in the basement. It was a totally secure area, with guns all over the wall of all shapes and sizes. I was allowed some target practice under supervision and fired a .38 and a big Magnum. The .38 was a piece of piss but the Magnum was mental and, when I pulled the trigger, I nearly blew a hole in the roof. I kid you not – when I fired it, I came close to shitting myself as a huge ball of fire came out of the barrel and the noise was deafening. It was far too powerful for me, hence it ended my introduction to firearms.

A few weeks later, I mentioned to Dave that I fancied another go with the Magnum and tried to convince him I'd be able to hit the target, not the roof! Dave told me in confidence that it was not going to happen as a day or two after I had visited the range he had been informed that he was not to take me there again due to my so-called 'connections' with the Liverpool underworld and, in particular, a family named the Bennetts.

The Bennetts! Where do I start? They are the family who allegedly ran me out of town, who slashed my legs or broke my ankles, depending on who is telling the story. In reality, that is utter bollocks as they were friends of mine when I was at Everton and are still friends of mine today. In fact, there is a picture in this book of me at Joey's 40th birthday party along with some other snaps from the old days, and what crazy days they were.

I first met Joey Bennett Snr when he worked on the door at the famous Conti Nightclub. It was a regular haunt of all the players and I got on really well with Joey and we became firm friends. Before long, I was introduced to his family and spent more time around their dinner table than I did around my own. They were down-to-earth and warm-hearted – my type of people.

Joey also worked at the docks and I loved going down there and meeting all the lads. I felt at home on the docks because of the working-class, salt-of-the-earth environment. I would often sit in the dockers' canteen and have a chat and laugh with the Scousers for hours.

After we beat Liverpool at Anfield thanks to Sharpy's goal of the season, I called at Joey's house and told him to get ready as we were going out to celebrate. As it happened, he had to work that night on the container base at Seaforth docks so we decided to nip down the docks, book him in and head to the Conti. For a laugh, I said I'd go and book him in while he waited in the car, so joined a huge queue of dockers.

They were all dressed in thick coats and hats wearing hob-nail boots and I looked a bit out of place wearing a smart suit ready for a nightclub! Soon, a few dockers recognised me and sussed what we were doing; they found it surreal that an Everton player was calling in for a night shift on the waterfront. We had a great laugh waiting to book in. Gradually, I got to the front and met the time-keeper who booked all the lads in and I calmly gave him Joey's number, 572. He looked up at me and blurted out in a broad Scouse accent, 'Who the fuck do you think you are with your London accent and smart-arse suit? I know whose number you have given me, and you're not Joey Bennett!'

The bloke did not have a clue that a few hours earlier I had played in a famous Everton win at Anfield and the other dockers were in fits of laughter. He clicked who I was and, luckily, he was an Evertonian so booked Joey in and told me to get him back for 3.00am as that was when the ship docked!

On the way to the Conti, I appreciated that the talent I had meant I did not have to queue for real and work a nightshift on the docks. Sadly, I did not always appreciate how lucky I was. We had a great time, the club was bouncing that night as the rest of the squad were there and they could not believe I had been down to the docks to put a shift in.

I used to meet up with Joey and his pal Tommy Hobart and go down to Paddy's Gym on Shaw Street where they did some sparring and bag work. One day, Joey must have been in a bad mood as he nearly knocked the bag through the wall. I remember Tommy saying to me that if Joey had caught me with that punch I would have been out for about three seasons; I told him I was just thinking the same thing. Joey's brothers – Tommy, Mickey, Sammy and Tony – were sparring, they were all excellent boxers and I was given the option of who I fancied a round or two with. My reply of 'None of you ... I'll see you in the pub later ...' raised a smile. I loved going to that gym; it was like being in a movie set in the Bronx, New York, a fantastic place.

Before the first Merseyside Cup Final I sorted Joey some tickets out and he picked them up from me at the training ground. I asked him where he was off to and he said the pub, so I jumped in with him and Tommy. We had to call at Goodison as Tommy had a season ticket and needed to collect his Cup Final ticket from the Goodison Road box office. When we got there, the queue was about a mile long and stretched down Walton Hall Avenue. Joey commented that we'd miss last orders, so I got Tommy's season ticket, went through the players' lounge and sorted it in two minutes. To celebrate, we went on a bender and I stayed out for a couple of nights.

I called in at Joey's house a bit worse for wear and he told me that Kevin Ratcliffe had been on the phone asking if he'd seen me, as the last time I had been spotted was getting in his car. Joey's wife Jean came in and gave me a bollocking, telling me to get back to Everton and to stop giving her husband a bad name.

Joey and his family were my guests at the 1986 Cup Final party in the Grosvenor Hotel where we had a great night, even though we lost the cup. The players had arranged a bar for friends and family where the drinks were cheaper, so I told Joey to get a round in for the lads while I went to the toilet. Unfortunately, he went to the wrong bar, and I was stung with an £80 tab for 16 pints of lager.

The Bennetts were mad Evertonians, so the day I was called up for the Welsh squad I got Rushy to phone Joey and tell him that I was his new team-mate and was proudly wearing a red shirt. Joey was going nuts until he heard us pissing ourselves laughing and he sussed it was a Wales shirt, not a Liverpool one!

Every Monday evening there was a family night at Bernie's Inn and I religiously joined the Bennett clan for a meal. The first time we went there the waitress approached us to take the order and I asked for a fillet steak. She asked how I would like it cooked so I replied, 'Edible ... two flips ... that's it!' I insisted that I didn't want anything else – no vegetables, potatoes, side orders, nothing, just the steak and a pint of lager.

She looked very bemused and the family thought it was hilarious, but that's all I ever had in such places. The meal arrived, a blood-covered steak and a pint of lager. I demolished it and told the waitress that it was delicious. The same thing happened for the next few visits – every time it was the same waitress and the same order. Eventually, she stopped asking me what I wanted and would just say 'same again for soft lad'. After weeks of this happening, the chef popped his head out of the serving hatch and asked the waitress, 'Where is he?' She pointed to me and he shouted, 'Fucking hell ... is it you? No wonder they call you Psycho Pat!'

One day, myself and Joey and his young son were driving along Dock Road when I saw an old tramp sitting on a cardboard box on the floor. I stopped the car, approached the man and handed him a £20 note, which in those days was a decent amount. I went over to the nearby café caravan and gave the lady who was serving another £20 asking her would she would make sure that the tramp would be fed and watered for the next 20 days as there was a huge sign advertising '£1 for tea, soup and a roll'. I returned to the car and said something like 'any one of us could end up like that …' and thought nothing more of it. Twenty years later, at his 40th, young Joey reminded me of that incident and told me he was so touched by my gesture that he would never forget it. I was amazed he remembered it, and it showed that even as a young lad he had respect for everyone.

On his 18th birthday, Joey Jnr bumped into me at the Conti and, at throwing out time, some of his mates invited me to join them at a 'rave' in Sefton Park. I was hesitant as I was wearing suit and also it was not really the kind of event footballers should be attending. After a minute of mild persuasion, one of the lads gave me a cap and a denim jacket to wear and off we went. We were having a good time when this big bloke recognised me and started to give me a bit of stick. It got out of hand and came close to blows before it settled down when the bloke apologised. I accepted his apology, even though I was still fuming as he was bang out of order.

We continued to enjoy ourselves but one of the lads who was in our company needed the toilet, which was a right hike across the park, so he simply pulled his zipper down and pissed all over this unused BBQ, which was situated next to where we stood.

Half an hour went by when, to our amusement, some-body came and lit the BBQ and started selling burgers. Revenge was sweet when the first customer to buy one was none other than the bloke who had given me grief earlier. That made our night.

In 1986, young Joey was playing for Liverpool schoolboys who had a few Everton fans in the side, one of them being Steve McManaman, who went on to have a great career. During a visit to Joey's house, the young Macca was there when I walked in, and he was a bit star-struck and asked for my autograph.

A few years later when I had joined Spurs, McManaman had got into the Liverpool first team and we were playing them at Anfield, so Joey turned up at The Moat House hotel to get some tickets for the game. He told me about Steve's progress and reminded me that he was his mate from all those years ago and laughed that I may want his autograph now. I replied, 'Mate or no mate – if he goes past me, I will kick him. Why's a good fucking Blue playing for them?'

Young Joey was actually on Everton's books as a kid and I often wonder, as does his father, if the rumours that swept the city had anything to do with him being released by the club. The rumours were nonsense and the reason I left Everton were purely personal and had nothing to do with problems in the city with the Bennetts or any other family either. As I have said, they were great friends of mine when I was at Everton and they still are today.

I did fear for my safety once when Joey Snr phoned and

told me to get my arse around to their house pronto. I had no idea what I had done wrong and was truly shitting myself when I arrived there. I walked into the front room and Joey was sitting around the table with some friends, Les and Joan Powell. They proceeded to hand me their latest telephone bill, which was an astonishing £650 for a quarter.

I then had a horrible flash-back to a couple of months earlier when I had gone to a local pub with Joey and some family friends, including Les and Joan. We had ended up back at the Powells' for a party and, when everyone had gone to bed, I crashed out on the couch. After a few minutes, I began thinking of Kimberly Cusack, a girl I had met on tour in Hawaii, so decided to phone her. I must have been on the blower to her for about three hours! In my drunken state, I had thought nothing of it, but weeks later the phone bill was a sobering reminder.

Joey just said, 'What are you going to do about this?'

I looked at Les and Joan and said, 'Will you take a cheque?' I paid the bill and we had a good laugh about it, although I was not invited to stop over at the Powells' ever again.

I hadn't long left Everton when I met Mandy Smith and was being driven around London one day in a Rolls-Royce drinking champagne, so I got Mandy to phone Joey and told her to invite him and Jean down for a weekend. They thought I was nuts and did not have a clue who she was. Before long, I wished I hadn't heard of her either.

The likes of John Smith, Tony Unghi and the Bennetts made my time in Liverpool extremely enjoyable. In fact, one of the main reasons I had to leave was that they were too enjoyable!

I was born in Belgium, raised in Millwall and played for Wales ... but my heart is 100 per cent Scouse!

8

A MATTER OF
LIFE AND DEATH

While we were still celebrating the most memorable season in Everton's proud history, disaster struck. The trouble at the Heysel stadium has been well documented and the tragic events that occurred on the 29 May 1985 – when 39 spectators, nearly all of them Juventus fans, were killed when a surge of Liverpool fans caused a wall to collapse at the European Cup final in Brussels – was, of course, a tragic event. However, for the life of me, I still cannot get my nut around the fact that somehow Everton were denied the opportunity to play in the same competition the following season.

I can't even recall where I was the day UEFA placed an indefinite ban on all English clubs in European competitions, with a proposition that Liverpool had to serve an extra three years once the ban was lifted. I was shell-shocked. What had we done wrong? What had the other clubs who had qualified for Europe done wrong? We were being denied the right to compete against the best sides in Europe, while Manchester United lost their place in the European Cup Winners' Cup and Tottenham Hotspur, Southampton and Norwich City were forced out of the UEFA Cup.

We were given some hope when all five clubs, including Everton, suggested they would appeal against the blanket ban on English clubs, feeling that only Liverpool should be penalised as it was their fans who'd rioted at Heysel. That was spot on, yes – ban Liverpool, despite them blaming everyone bar themselves for the trouble, but let the rest of us who had done no wrong compete in competitions as we had earned the right to.

The appeals, not surprisingly, fell on deaf ears and, having been so ecstatic at the end of the season and looking forward to the new one with such excitement, before we had even gone on holiday we had been dumped on from a great height. UEFA and Mrs Thatcher's knee-jerking Government wanted scapegoats, Everton were therefore denied the chance to push on for bigger and better honours. Nobody, no matter how hard they try, will ever convince me that the FA, UEFA or the British Government made the right decision banning us, a decision that affected Everton Football Club more than any other club. I'm told Liverpool fans say Everton are bitter towards them because of it; I believe they have every right to be, and if that pisses them off, then so be it.

As well as the supporters, it hurt us, the players, immensely. All the lads were looking forward to playing in the European Cup following our success in the Cup Winners' Cup the previous season. Why ban Everton? Of course, we had our fair share of problematic fans, every club did, but in Rotterdam they were fantastic and a credit to Everton Football Club, Merseyside and indeed to British football. Evertonians deserved to be treated better by the so-called governing body of our great game. We were let down badly by those people who took an easy option. Many people say Everton never recovered from it and I myself take that view. Maybe we would have been knocked out in the first round, but not to be given the chance to compete, through no fault of our own, was a bitter pill to swallow.

Deep down, although Howard stayed on for two more seasons after Heysel, I think his reasons for leaving were generally because of the European ban. Remember, when we regained the title in 1987, once again we were denied the right to compete against Europe's finest.

So after the end-of-season celebrations, the dreadful scenes at Heysel and the usual, crazy close-season tour, we were back at Bellfield for a tough pre-season. We were greeted by a new face as, on 1 August, Everton signed 24-year-old Leicester City and England striker Gary Lineker for a club record fee of £900,000. Gary was brought in to replace Andy Gray whom Howard had controversially sold to Aston Villa during the close season. I was sorry to see Andy go, he was a great player and superb in the dressing room, but I think by signing Lineker, Howard was setting his stall out. He was letting the other top clubs know that we were not sitting on our past glory and were looking to push on. Nobody saw it coming and it was a shame Andy never had his chance to say goodbye to the lads and the fans as he did as much as anybody to turn the fortunes of the club around. Along with Peter Reid, he was regarded as one of the two signings who saved Howard from being sacked when things were not going well for him.

We began the season back at Wembley where we beat Manchester United in the Charity Shield. I was not a lover of the fixture; OK, it was at Wembley, but I always viewed it as another game in which to get match fit before the real business began. We beat them 2–0 but the most important thing was the return of Adrian Heath who came on as a sub and scored.

Inchy had missed all the glory in May when we were lifting the cups but, without his goals early on in the season, we may not have won anything. Although he'd missed out, it was great to see him back playing, as some thought the injury he suffered may have ended his career.

The fixture computer set up an opening game with a twist – Leicester away for Lineker's début – and we duly got slammed 3–1. Knowing Andy Gray as well as I do, I bet he pissed himself laughing when that score came through. We soon settled, Links started finding the net and we were up to second in the league before we visited QPR, the scene of my sending-off the previous year. For the second time in a few weeks, we were hammered, this time 3–0. It was the worst defeat I had suffered since joining Everton and already people were questioning Howard's decision to sell Gray as our style of play had changed quite a bit.

Although it was just a straight swap, a striker for a striker, we had already started to go a little 'route one' as Lineker's pace gave us that option. We were never told to play that way but, in the past, it was pointless humping the ball over the opposition back four as, unless Andy Gray booked a taxi or Sharpy got on the end of it, the ball would invariably come straight back at us. With Lineker giving chase, it gave you time to regroup and settle. Such was his pace, more often than not he would get to the ball or at the very least force a defender to concede a throw-in or corner. This was all well and good, but the game started by-passing the midfield lads and, at times, you could see them getting frustrated as the ball sailed over their heads. It wasn't route one Wimbledon, but hardly the Everton who had footballed teams off the park just a season earlier.

Even at that early stage of the season, it looked like we may struggle to retain the title as Manchester United were on fire and were top of the First Division with a 100 per cent record after 10 games. We beat them 4–2 at Old Trafford although, sadly, it was in a pointless competition called the Screen Sport Super Cup, which was arranged to compensate us for not playing in Europe. It was an absolute joke, a total waste of time and a drain on the fans' wages.

Just a few weeks into the season, injuries started to take

their toll. Derek Mountfield was struggling and eventually missed about half the season until he regained full fitness and, at the same time, we lost Reidy for over 30 games. Both were top players, Reid was an inspiration and Mountfield, as well as being a decent defender, scored as many goals as most strikers did. To lose them both at the same time was a massive headache for the gaffer.

Things hit rock bottom when we trudged off the pitch at half-time 3–0 down to Liverpool at a shocked Goodison Park. Ian Marshall had come in for Mountfield and we were torn to pieces by Liverpool in the first half. Howard pulled Marshall at the interval and we went for it in the second half and came so close to getting a draw after Lineker and Sharpy had got it back to 3–2. Despite getting nothing from the game points wise, that second half showing gave us a massive confidence boost. Although we never really hit the form of the previous season, we regrouped and picked up enough points to keep us in touch of United and the other side above us, who sadly came from across the park.

Howard pulled me to one side in training and asked whether I'd be happy to go into the centre of defence alongside Rats as it had been confirmed that Derek would be out for some considerable time. I was more than happy to oblige; I had always seen that position as my best but told the gaffer that although I was happy to take over from Mountfield in defence, not to expect me to push Lineker for the Golden Boot award. I knew my limitations. I asked Howard who would play left-back as, sadly, Bails was out of favour, and he told me to concentrate on my own job in hand and let him do his.

The following day Everton signed 21-year-old Neil Pointon with the left-back joining us from Scunthorpe for a bargain £75,000. I never felt threatened by his arrival; I knew if I played well and kept out of trouble I would play more games for Everton than I missed. I managed to achieve one of those requirements reasonably well!

My positional change got off to a shaky start and we lost two out of the three league games I played there. I missed the next game at home to Arsenal when Pointon came in at left-back; Gary Stevens went alongside Ratcliffe and I was sat in the stands as we humiliated the Gunners 6–1. It was an awesome display and I did think that maybe I would be frozen out, such was the quality on the park that day. Howard put my mind at rest and I was recalled at left-back for an away win at Ipswich. We then went seven games unbeaten with an easy 3–0 win at West Brom, a game in which I scored and joked to Howard that I was only 15 behind Lineker!

Howard once again pulled me and said that Pointon was going to slot in at left-back and that I would move back across to the centre as he had tried almost every back four formation and he saw that as his strongest. I was just happy to be playing. It was the most open title race for years as United had dropped a few points and the likes of West Ham and Chelsea were on good runs, so with ourselves and Liverpool it was looking like anybody's title.

I picked up a knock in a League Cup defeat at home to

Chelsea and missed the return game with Leicester at Goodison the following Saturday. Once again, they did us, leaving with a 2–1 win and how those two defeats to a side struggling near the relegation zone would cost us come May.

We had dropped to sixth in the league but the gaffer told us that we had four games in ten days over the festive period which would make or break our season, and we won three of them, including a home victory over leaders United. A draw at Newcastle on New Year's Day took us up to second and that was the start of a run of about 20 games unbeaten. One of these games saw me make my return to St Andrew's when we beat my old side 2–0 thanks to a brace from Lineker. Birmingham were really struggling and there were just over 10,000 in the crowd and, with the way they were playing and the lack of support they were getting, it was no real surprise when they were relegated weeks before the season ended.

For our next league game we welcomed back Peter Reid, who scored our goal in the 1–0 victory over Spurs as we went top for the first time that season. United were dropping points left, right and centre but Liverpool were also taking advantage of the situation and were always within a couple of points of us. The Derby at Anfield was a week away and that gave us a chance to pull clear of them. We did just that after nipping across the park and coming back home happy, having won 2–0. I went home sore from that game after Kevin Ratcliffe had KO'd me when a ball went over the top and Rats thought I was not going to make it and cleaned me out, as well as clearing the danger. I looked like I had been hit by a runaway train.

As well as a great reader of the game with amazing pace, he was a tough defender and amazed everyone in that game when he scored from about 20 yards with a net-buster past Bruce Grobbelaar. OK, it may not have hit the net as hard as Sharp's volley the season before, but it crossed the line and, for two years running, we beat the Reds in their own back yard. Howard got the two of us together after the game and congratulated us on the way we played together, once again letting me know that he rated me as a centre-back.

Despite the win at Anfield, there was little margin for error as it was tight at the top of the league and, although our run-in was reasonable, we had a few tricky away games. One I never fancied was at Luton on that joke of a plastic pitch they were somehow allowed to play on. Before heading to Kenilworth Road, we hosted Chelsea who, alongside Liverpool, were pushing us all the way for the title. They had beaten us at their place 2–1 in a game that saw Neville sent off when he carried the ball out of the area in mid-flight, a ridiculous decision that once again cost us dearly. Chelsea took a point off us at Goodison and we stayed top but, once again, struggled on the plastic surface and were beaten 2–1 by Luton.

A few days later, Nev broke his ankle playing in a pointless game for Wales and I really began to think that our luck had deserted us and that maybe this was not to be our season. On the plus side, Bobby Mimms, Nev's deputy, was a great 'keeper and Mountfield and Reid were fit again, although Kevin Sheedy picked up an injury on the plastic pitch that saw him miss the run-in. Mimms did brilliantly and kept a remarkable six clean sheets on the bounce to put us within touching distance of regaining the title as, despite Liverpool leading the table on goal difference from us, we had the all-important game in hand.

We were not conceding but Lineker's goals had dried up and, although we beat Newcastle at home, we came away from Old Trafford and Nottingham Forest with a point from each after two uneventful goalless draws. We then travelled to Oxford that mid-week knowing that the points dropped at the City Ground could cost us dearly if we failed to get something at the Manor Ground.

It was a game from hell. We missed chance after chance and, as so often is the case, despite not being in the game, Oxford stole a late winner. After the game, Links commented that the wrong boots had been packed for the trip and the press made a bit of a thing about it in the papers and tried to apportion the blame on a member of staff. To me that was bollocks – if a certain pair of boots are so precious, you should pack them yourself. Gary was obviously disappointed with the defeat and the chances he missed, but sometimes you have to hold your hands up and admit to having an off day.

The defeat gave Liverpool the chance to clinch the Championship at Chelsea the following Saturday and, although we thrashed Southampton 6–1 on the same day, they took it, winning 1–0 at Stamford Bridge. Occasionally, we would get a reaction from the crowd that gave us hope that the game at Chelsea was going our way, but they were Chinese whispers. Deep down, everyone knew that we had handed Liverpool the title a few days earlier and that they were not going to give it us back.

Everton completed the season and finished runners-up to our greatest rivals with a 3–1 win against West Ham. I was totally deflated; I had played more games than any player at the club that season, trained hard, kept myself fit, free from injury and, more importantly, stayed out of trouble … and ended up with nothing.

I talk to people now about that heartbreaking season and they still blame the style of play. Although Lineker scored 30 league goals, a superb achievement, they dried up in other areas and maybe that was down to playing it long to Gary. One thing I will not blame it on is the fact that somebody packed the wrong boots for our star striker – in reality, we only had ourselves to blame.

Quite simply, if you lose twice to Leicester and at the likes of Oxford and Luton, do you really deserve to be crowned champions? I'd say no.

9

A LEAGUE OF
THEIR OWN

I began pre-season training still on a downer, as losing out on the Double to your local rivals – and I'm being very polite calling them that – as well as being wrongly deprived of competing in Europe the previous season was as bad as it could get. We also said goodbye to our star striker Gary Lineker, who left us after just one season to join Barcelona. I was sorry to see him go as his goals ratio was as good as it gets and that was endorsed when he won the Golden Boot that summer at the World Cup finals in Mexico.

Personally, I think Lineker owed us another season. Everton had put him in the spotlight; the likes of Barcelona probably would not have gone for him had he still been at Leicester and, although we got good money for Gary, I think he jumped ship a bit quick. There was talk of Howard joining him and we were glad he turned down a couple of approaches and stayed loyal to us. I just hoped Gary remembered to pack his lucky boots before getting on the plane to Barça.

With money burning a hole in Howard's pocket, he chose to spend it wisely and, although his signings that season were not headline news, they were all were very clever additions to the squad. He spent the Lineker money on Neil Adams, Wayne Clarke, Kevin Langley, Paul Power, Ian Snodin and Dave Watson, while Warren Aspinall, Kevin Richardson and Paul Wilkinson all made for the exit.

I was sorry to see Richardson leave for Watford; he was a quality player and a superb squad member at Everton. Had he been playing for nearly any other side at that time, he would have been a first-team regular. He never once let us down when he came in for lads who were suspended or injured, and also scored some vital goals for us. The move to Vicarage Road was seen as a step down, but it was no surprise when a couple of years later he won another League Championship medal with Arsenal and, knowing Kevin, it was made even more special when they won it at Anfield.

The signing of Manchester City veteran Paul Power raised a few eyebrows as he was at the wrong end of his career; however, Howard knew that we needed back-up in defence as, apart from a few lads still nursing minor knocks, Derek Mountfield was a long-term casualty and one dickhead – me – was out for months after a stupid fight in a local nightclub.

The problem began when I borrowed £50 from two well-known local brothers while out in town one night and, for one reason or another, I never gave it them back. What a costly mistake that would turn out to be. I had visited a local Chinese with the squad for a club-organised team meeting and then moved on to a favourite watering hole for a few beers with the usual suspects.

I can remember having a few words with Steve McMahon in this pub after he had said something unpleasant about Howard Kendall. I could take or leave McMahon; he was a decent player and we had a few tussles on the pitch, but I did not take kindly to him slagging Howard off and told him so. Eventually, things calmed down, Steve left and a few of us stayed on playing pool and chatting to some birds who had tagged along with us.

Later that night, we moved to The Toad Hall in Ainsdale which was a well-known nightclub at the time. I was laughing and joking with a few of the lads when one of these girls who had tagged on to us said something unpleasant and caused a bit of a scene. I know now that it was a set-up, as the minute I tried to find out what her problem was some bloke came from nowhere and threw the head on me. We ended up brawling over a table so I got him in a headlock and, as quickly as it had started, it was over. We were getting ready to leave when Inchy noticed my leg was pissing with blood so the lads got me into his car and we set off to the nearest hospital. All the way there, he was moaning that there was blood gushing from my leg on to his seats and he kept telling me that I was going to have to pay for it to be cleaned!

I was examined and the medical staff were not sure if I had fallen on glass or had been stabbed with a bottle; either way, it was a nasty cut that required seven stitches to tidy it up. I limped into Bellfield the next morning and told anyone daft enough to listen to me that I had been walking my dog on the beach and had fallen on some glass causing the injury, which might keep me out for a few weeks. I don't for one minute think anyone believed me, but it was the best I could come up with at the time. A few weeks turned into a few months and it was a long road back to fitness, with one complication after another preventing my road to recovery. By the time I was ready to play, I had missed almost six months of a soon-to-be-memorable season.

After several failed attempts, I eventually made my comeback in an FA Cup tie at Bradford after I had made about half-a-dozen reserve appearances. I then made my first league start of the season a week later, when we beat Coventry to go top for the first time that term. The team obviously needed me!

It was a frustrating time for me as I would play a game here and a game there before I'd pick up another niggle or fresh injury. In total, I ended up playing only seven full games all season, which was a nightmare.

Following the Coventry win we went to Oxford, the team who had beaten us a year earlier, a defeat which had cost us the Championship. It was a case of déjà vu as we went 1–0 down, but Paul Wilkinson scored very late on to earn us a massive point to keep us in top spot. A couple of weeks later, Paul moved to Nottingham Forest, which I found strange as he was getting games, scoring goals and was in with a chance of winning the biggest medal in English League football.

We were not playing as well as we had done in previous seasons but were winning games while others were dropping points so it was really a two-horse race between ourselves and Liverpool. Our home form was excellent and Goodison was a fortress where we only lost once all season. On the road was a different matter as we lost seven, including games against Watford, Charlton, Forest and West Ham, teams we should really have been beating. The defeat at Watford cost us top spot and gave Liverpool the edge again but, like us, they were not on top form and dropped points against teams they should have been beating.

The run-in was difficult with back-to-back games at Arsenal and Chelsea. I played in the one at Highbury when Wayne Clarke chipped the Arsenal 'keeper from about 30 yards and the same day Wimbledon won at Anfield to make us favourites.

Clarke was another great signing by Howard. Sharpy, like myself, was struggling with injury and, although I don't think Wayne was anywhere near as good as Graeme, he came in and scored some really important goals for us.

By now, after a shaky start, Dave Watson had won the Goodison faithful over. It was never going to be easy for Waggy as he had previously played for Liverpool and was replacing huge crowd favourite Derek Mountfield who, like myself, missed the majority of the season through injury, although his absence was football related. Watson was a rock for us and rightly went on to become a huge player for Everton; when you were up against it, he was someone you would want alongside you.

The same went for another of Howard's signings – Ian Snodin – as with Paul Bracewell out for the season we needed quality back-up and Snodds gave us that. May I also say he fitted into the social side of things at the club perfectly. Ian had to choose between us and Liverpool and very few people turned down a move to Anfield, and I often wonder if he had joined them instead of us whether the title race would have had the same outcome.

Once again I was injured, but we won at Chelsea thanks to goals from Waggy and Alan Harper, then beat West Ham at home before two massive wins over the Easter period meant we had one hand on the title. We came away from Villa Park with a 1–0 victory, before beating Newcastle at Goodison two days later thanks to a Clarke hat-trick. I missed most of the run-in, including the game against Liverpool, when they opened the title up slightly by beating us 3–1 at Anfield, but was back for a disappointing home draw against Manchester City, a side that were looking like relegation certs. In the dressing room after the game, news came through that Liverpool had been beaten at Coventry City, meaning that we could clinch our second League title in three years by winning at Norwich on the Bank Holiday Monday.

Carrow Road was not really a happy hunting ground for us as I had been pulled off during a 4–2 hammering the season we had won our first Championship. Even though they were relegated, which was down to us losing at Coventry on the last game of the season, we had to go there the following campaign to play in some stupid, worthless cup game when we were beaten again. Although the stakes were a lot higher this time, it was going to be a tough game as they were a very good side at home.

We, and myself in particular, got off to the perfect start. We forced a corner direct from the kick-off and, after less than a minute, I connected with a Trevor Steven cross and thumped an unstoppable shot into the top corner … albeit from about 3 yards out! Even from that range, I would not have put money on myself hitting the target; nine times out of ten somebody in the crowd would have caught the ball but fortunately I connected well and am down in the record books as the man who won Everton the league. I, like the rest of the players, got carried to the dressing room on the shoulders of Evertonians who filled the Carrow Road pitch at the final whistle. I was a hero!

Seriously, I do not see it that way – my input that season was barely worth a mention but it was nice to get such an important goal and what a celebration we had on the way home. It could not have been any better as there were motorway jams, such was the volume of traffic heading back to Merseyside, and nobody cared if it took us all night to get home. It was a fantastic feeling winning the title back from our bitterest rivals who had broken my heart the previous season. It was back to business as usual!

We were presented with the Championship Trophy after the home game against Luton which we won 3–1 thanks to two Trevor Steven penalties. I was a little disappointed that after my net-bursting strike at Norwich that I hadn't been asked to take them!

Everton completed the season with another home win against Spurs when a couple of lads played – Neil Adams was one – meaning they qualified for a medal. Derek Mountfield was another and we were all delighted for him when he scored the winner that day as his season, like mine, had been an injury-plagued nightmare. We eventually finished nine points clear of runners-up Liverpool and I was fortunate enough to have made the required amount of appearances also to secure a winner's medal. Did I deserve one? Given the pain and suffering I went though before making my comeback and the fact I hit the net with that 3-yard screamer at Norwich, too right I did!

10

WHAT HAPPENS ON TOUR ...

After moving to Everton, I was always being told by the players that at the end of the season we all go on holiday together, and they emphasised the word 'holiday'. I was not sure if it was just for a piss-up or to conclude a club-organised tour or as a team bonding exercise but, whatever the reason, Mr Kendall thought it was a good way to finish off the season. Who were we to argue? After all, he was the gaffer.

The trips went down in Goodison folklore, usually for all the wrong reasons. There is, however, no doubt in my mind that Howard's way was the right way as the team spirit was better at Everton than anywhere else I had played or would play later in my career. Spain was always the favourite destination and that was the case after my first season; as promised, the fine from my sending off at Queen's Park Rangers was in the beer kitty, along with cash collected from the other players who had either broken club rules or been booked or sent off during the season.

On the first day, I went out with the lads and we drank the place dry. It was fantastic. We had just finished a great season and were rightly allowed to let our hair down a bit. My lasting memory of this holiday was walking back to the hotel and chatting away to Sharpy when, after a minute or so, I looked around and realised he was missing. I was pissed but not quite pissed enough to have lost a big bloke like him, and then noticed Terry Darracott and Colin Harvey sitting in a bar facing the direction I had just come from. They asked me if I was OK, and I said I was fine, but had lost my drinking buddy Sharpy. Without an ounce of concern, one of them said, 'He's just fallen into that big bush over there ... he'll be OK!' With that they carried on drinking.

I was gobsmacked. Sharpy was a top player, worth probably a couple of million in those days, and the assistant manager and head coach were not too concerned that he had just gone arse over tit into a huge bush in the middle of a busy seaside resort. I walked back and indeed, there he was. I helped him up and we continued our walk back to the hotel as if nothing had happened. I was learning quickly about life at Everton.

Of course, with holidays and the beer come the birds ... and there were plenty of them hovering about when there were footballers in town. One night, I was out with a member of the club, not a player but a well-respected employee, who was always there if we needed him. Not a minder as such, but someone the club knew could handle himself and who was also responsible enough to keep an eye on things to ensure things never got too out of control.

I did not really know what the situation was with bringing birds back to the hotel – was it a line that was not to be crossed? The majority of the players were just happy with the beer, so I never pushed my luck too much. This particular night as we walked down the corridor, I noticed one of the lad's doors was open and, as you do, I put my head in for a nose. The player was fast asleep with three naked girls strewn across his room.

I tip-toed in and could see that they had all been previously enjoying themselves. One woke up and immediately set about pulling my shorts down. One thing led to another, but I refused to go too far as I knew she had already been seen to and had not showered, so I settled for a lower massage and eventually shot my load. The girl had a good grip on me but my team-mate ended up getting something across his head that he was not too happy about when he came down for breakfast the following morning. Although he was never 100 per cent certain it was me, he gave me a look to let me know he had a good idea that it was.

Believe it or not, at this stage of my Everton career I was on my best behaviour. Now that may not have been as good as some people would expect, but it was as good as it gets. One example came a few nights later when a couple of us hooked up with a group of girls in some club and the one I sat with would not let me near her. All she kept saying was, 'No … let's go back to your room.' Now that's about right if you're having a little play, a bit of a kiss and cuddle and getting a bit worked up. But this girl was not letting me even hold hands with her, so I smelt a rat and fucked her off.

A year later, on the eve of the Cup Final against Liverpool, I got a call from reception informing me that there was a lady asking for me in the hotel, so I went for a look and it was her. Once again she was saying, 'Please let's go to your room …'

To this day, I don't know if she intended to rob me, sell her story to the papers or quite simply was really shy and only performed in a private room with the lights off! As I said, I was not off the rails at that time so never found out and, once again, told her to fuck off. Had she returned a year or so later, I may not have been so suspicious.

I soon got settled at Everton and came out of my shell a bit, none so more than when we flew to New Zealand via LA and Australia. We got absolutely steaming on the flight and, when we landed in America, we were all escorted off the plane and taken to security where we were warned that we may be sent home once we had sobered up. It appears, although I can't remember the incident, that I had walked from the front of the aircraft to the back of it with my cock out. I won't argue with the people who said I did, as it was something I had done before at Birmingham. If it is true, I can only apologise to anybody offended and appreciate they did not take pictures and sell them to the papers as, in all honesty, it's not a Championship-winning part of my anatomy!

Eventually, we ended up in Australia and, as usual, we ended up clubbing, but this night I got lucky when I was introduced to a gorgeous model. I thought I was in for the night of my life until this bloke came over and it was obvious that he was this stunner's partner. He was a very polite young man and, in passing, I asked him what he did and he replied rather cockily that he, too, was a model. Fuck me, I thought, it's Ken and Barbie!

He then got a little bit complacent and left us alone and went off chatting to a gang of girls at the other side of the club. His bird was a bit pissed off so I seized my chance and asked her would she like to dance and she agreed. I held her hand and took her to the furthest corner of the club, away from her posing boyfriend, and we held hands and chatted for ages. I knew she had either fallen for my charms or was looking to get her own back on her pretty-boy partner – either was fine with me.

Just before the club closed, Ken appeared and caught us sitting a little bit close to each other and immediately asked me what the fuck I was playing at. I told him very politely that we were just chatting, but he was having none of it and grabbed the girl's arm, informing her that they were leaving. She pushed him away and just said, 'No, I'm going home with him!'

He looked at me and I looked at him and could not help but throw him a sly smirk. He was a big-headed clown and had come unstuck, so he muttered something and left us to it. Within an hour, we had arrived at her flat and it was an experience, to put it mildly. She led me to the bedroom and we undressed each other before I climbed on to this huge bed which I soon realised was actually a water bed. I had never sat on such a contraption before, never mind done the business on one, so I just lay there while she got herself ready and joined me. I was lying too near the edge, so when she joined me she caused a bit of a wave and, before I knew it, I'd been thrown off and was now bollock-naked on the floor. Once I got back on, we had an absolutely hilarious time and, although I would not rate it as my best ever sexual experience, it was 100 per cent the funniest.

We finished the tour in New Zealand and I ended up taking another girl back to my room, where I knew the beds were normal. My room-mate was fast asleep, so we started having a bit of a play when, all of a sudden, there was a knock on the door. I was once again bollock-naked, so my team-mate jumped up and foolishly opened the door without asking who was outside. As soon as the door opened, in walked this bird's husband – he was a big bastard, too. So there I was, lying in bed with his wife, and he's just standing there looking as if he's ready to kill us both. He never uttered a single word, just stared at us for what seemed like an hour – although it was probably less than a minute – shook his head and walked out. She got dressed and left and, from that night on, it was always an unwritten rule that you had to ask who was knocking before ever opening the door to them, especially if you had a bird in bed with you!

A couple of seasons later, we went on an end-of-season trip to Hawaii, which nearly brought a premature end to my football career. Myself and Gary Stevens unpacked and headed straight for Waikiki Beach and got ourselves a beer. Once again, things could not get any better ... and then I set eyes on Kimberly Cusack. I first noticed her standing by this little beach bar talking to Paul Power, so I wandered over and introduced myself and asked her if she'd like a drink. She declined quite bluntly, before telling me she was only 17 and hence not allowed to drink alcohol. I was stumped, so the best I could come out with was, 'Fancy a swim?'

For sure, it was not the best chat-up line I ever came out with, but it worked as she looked me in the eye and said softly, 'I'd love to.' As we walked towards the water, she held my hand and we ended up chatting for hours. We never left the water; I was totally besotted with her and she was the most beautiful thing I had ever set eyes on. We splashed about and chatted some more, then I noticed that it was nearly dark and that everyone had left and we were the only ones still on the beach.

We dried off and then went to few bars and eventually ended up in her friend's apartment where we shared some Southern Comfort and a couple of spliffs. Now, I was never much good after the wacky baccy so I could hardly stand up, but still managed to do the business throughout the night. She was electric and we did it in the shower, over the sink and every place and position we could think of. Miss Cusack was quite simply fantastic in every way possible and Mr Van Den Hauwe had fallen for her, as always, hook, line and sinker.

I never saw a single player for the duration of the trip and was with Kimberly 24 hours a day until the final day when we were due to fly home. I had made my mind up – I was staying, fuck football, this was the life for me. I went and saw Howard and told him I would like to stay for another week's holiday, but he told me we had arrived as a team and would leave as one. Deep down, I think he knew I had fallen for this girl as nobody had seen sight or sound of me for a week. He was probably doing his best to get me away from her, for the good of myself, the club and also my marriage, something I had not got round to telling the delightful Miss Cusack about.

I went and told Kimberly that I had to go home but she said I was welcome to return to Alaska with her and work on her father's ranch. It was foolish talk, but I swear I was going along with it, from a League Champion and international footballer to a ranch hand in one week – crazy, but it's what I had decided to do.

I went and saw Howard again and this time he was a little more serious about the matter and told me to get a grip and that I would be on the plane the following day. I went and found Kimberly, told her the bad news and, within seconds, she was gone. Had Howard allowed me to stay for another week, I would have never gone back; as soon as the plane had taken off, I'd have packed my bags and buggered off to Alaska with this 17-year-old girl I had fallen head over heels in love with.

Later that night, I was lying on the bed in my room resenting football and everything that came with it as I had discovered something that I found to be enjoyable. I was not giving a second thought to my poor wife at home or the repercussions my running off could have on my career and on the people who were close to me. I just wanted to spend all my time with this girl whom I'd only known for a week. As anyone who knew what I was like at the time would simply say, 'That's Pat Van Den Hauwe for you!'

At about 9.00pm there was a knock on the door and I was so pleased that it was Kimberly asking me to take a walk to the beach, not Big Nev asking me if I fancied a cup of tea! We walked to the spot we had first met and made love there and then and she promised to wait for me, telling me to do as the club said, then return as soon as I could and rejoin her. We spent a night in my room together before saying goodbye in the morning and I promised I would phone her every day until I could manage to get away from football and join her on her family ranch.

I swear, my phone bills nearly crippled me. I was spending hundreds of pounds every month calling her, I never tired of it. Then, one day, I asked her if she'd met anyone and she was honest and told me that she had been to a party and slept with a guy. She promised me it was a one-night stand and she still missed and loved me, but I was so angry I put the phone down on her and never spoke to her again.

I was told months later that she had been calling me at the club and had even sent a parcel that contained edible knickers and all sorts of photos of her, but they were all intercepted and

I never even got to have a photo of her as a keepsake. I don't know who the bloke was she slept with, but whoever he was, he saved my football career!

11

SWEET FA IN THE CUP

The day I signed my apprenticeship forms at St Andrew's, my father turned to me and said, 'Good luck, son ... one day I want to see you play in a Cup Final at Wembley. Don't let me down!' It was a tough ask and I bet it is something that every father wishes for when their son signs up as a professional footballer.

It was a few years before I had the chance to make his dream come true as I never played in a single FA Cup tie in my first five seasons at Birmingham, and I never missed much as we always seemed to go out of the competition early doors. That trend changed, however, when I was established in the side during the 1983/84 season.

I have always looked forward to the day of the FA Cup third-round draw. Even today, when the Cup has been somewhat devalued by some clubs who play under-strength sides in the early rounds, the third-round draw is special.

That season with Birmingham, we were drawn out of the hat with Sheffield United, a tough place to go at the best of times, but we managed to come away with a draw thanks to a Billy Wright penalty. The replay went to plan as we ran out 2–0 winners, thanks to another Wright spot-kick after Mick Harford had got our first.

The draw was again not kind to us and we had to travel up to Sunderland's old ground, Roker Park, on a freezing day in late January. I was up against Leighton James, a very experienced winger, but kept him under wraps and we were doing well until a clash of heads between Noel Blake and Ian Atkins held the game up for a while. Noel was hard as nails and, after he was sorted by the sponge man and re-took his position, it was no shock when their lad was taken off and did not return. A few minutes later, Billy Wright somehow got his head to a ball that was going wide and thundered a header into our net to give them a 1–0 lead at half-time. After the break, Tony Coton kept us in the game and, with a few minutes left, we equalised with a goal from midfielder Martin Kuhl. We were more than satisfied to take them back to our place but, with about a minute to go, Mick Harford won it for us and, for the first time ever, I wondered if this could be the year I made my father's dream come true.

At this stage of the competition, all we could ask for was a home draw, although West Ham at St Andrew's was not going to be easy as the Hammers were having their best season for years and were an established top-five outfit and were in great form. We, on the other hand, were once again struggling to avoid the dreaded drop into Division Two. The form book went out of the window and goals by Hopkins, Rees and another Billy Wright penalty had us all dreaming of Wembley.

A lot of top sides were by now out of the competition; in earlier rounds, the Cup holders Manchester United had lost at Bournemouth, Brighton had beaten favourites Liverpool and Spurs had gone out to Norwich, so ourselves, Plymouth, Watford, Notts County, Derby and Sheffield Wednesday were in the last eight, with new favourites Everton and Southampton. All the lads knew if we could avoid those two we were in with a great chance, especially if we were drawn at home.

We got what we hoped for, but then it all went horribly wrong as, in front of over 40,000 fans at a packed St Andrew's, we got swept away by a John Barnes-inspired Watford. It was yet another false dawn for the Blues and we were gutted. We had beaten them 2–0 at home in the league and, although they were a good side, they were lightweight and we knew if we got amongst them we'd be in with a great chance of reaching the semi-finals.

We never banked on John Barnes playing as well as he did and, after about half-an-hour, he swept past two of us and slotted in to give them the lead. We got back into the game when Steve Terry sent a cross into their box past his own 'keeper and I thought at that point that our name may well have been on the Cup. No chance, as we left their centre-back Taylor free to score and, late on, Barnes finished at the far post to send us crashing out. We really did think we had a chance that year and I was truly upset that day as I suffered FA Cup heartache for the first time. In my wildest dreams, I could not have known how much more heartache I would suffer in the competition before I eventually ended up with a winner's medal.

To make matters worse, Watford drew Plymouth in the semi-final draw, giving them a relatively easy route to the final. I'll admit that I was happy to see Everton beat them in the final, for no other reason than they had ruined my dream. I was not to know when I cheered Andy Gray and Graeme Sharp's goals that, because of Everton winning the Cup, I would help them compete in Europe the following season, having gained entry by beating Watford that day.

My first FA Cup tie for Everton was a tough one at Elland Road on another freezing night. The game had been switched from the usual Saturday afternoon slot to a Friday night to accommodate live TV and, although Leeds United were in the Second Division, they were still rated as a decent side. Before the game, the TV commentator reminded us all that we had not won at Elland Road for 30-odd years; thanks for that, I thought. It was another game when John Bailey gave way for me, as I had been covering at right-back for an injured Gary Stevens. With Gary fit, I moved to left-back and I could see that John was getting pissed off as he had played well when Gary had been out.

As much as it pissed Bails off, a manager has to live and die by making decisions and Howard made the right one as we beat Leeds and ended the 30-year-old hoodoo with a comfortable 2–0 victory. Sharpy put us one up before half-time with a disputed penalty and Sheeds finished them off when his late free kick hit the bar and, as everyone watched the ball, he followed it in and smashed the rebound into the net.

A relatively comfortable home win against a Doncaster side containing the Snodin brothers saw us make the last 32 and, once again, I was dreaming of the Twin Towers. To give Donny credit, they were a hard nut to crack and it was probably that game when the gaffer noticed that one of the Snodins was a half-decent footballer. A couple of years later, Ian signed for us and was a top player, whose career was sadly hampered by injury. That day, he was a bit lippy and I gave him a thump in the ear to pipe him down a bit, which didn't work, although goals from Stevens and Steven did!

The chance of my dream becoming reality was given a massive boost when we were paired with Alliance Premier League side Telford United, who had beaten Fourth Division promotion challengers Darlington 3–0 as we were seeing off Doncaster, to become only the fifth ever non-league side to progress that far in the competition.

Unlike Doncaster, who tried to play a bit of football and who were applauded off the pitch at full time by our appreciative fans, Telford were simply dirty bastards and came to kick us off the pitch. We had to dig in, show some grit and give them a bit back; it was like a war and turned out to be a very hard, physical game. They had a lad up front called Ken McKenna who was a massive Evertonian;

when he left his foot in early on, we knew they would all be at it. They were cheered on by the largest away following I had ever seen at Goodison, but second-half goals from Reidy, Trevor Steven and Sheeds shut them up a bit and, unlike Donny, they were booed off at full time as the home fans took exception to their spoiling and often brutal antics.

Don't get me wrong – I was no angel and loved a physical challenge, and appreciate that teams from the lower leagues have to play to their strengths, but I think the reaction of the Evertonians that day let them know they had overstepped the mark. Had they have seen some of the lads' legs in the dressing room after the game they would have had those views endorsed.

Yet another home tie gave us a great chance of making the semi-finals, as relegation-threatened Ipswich Town arrived at Goodison as huge underdogs. The form book went out of the window, as happens so often in the Cup and, despite Sheeds scoring with a famous free kick, we almost went out. The free kick was something I had never seen at any level and, to this day, I still haven't. It was classic Sheeds as he curled his shot from outside the box into the top right-hand corner, but was told to retake it, so he re-spotted the ball and simply put it in the top left-hand corner!

Despite Kevin's genius with a minute to go, we found ourselves 2–1 down and it was manic as we chased the all-important second goal needed to keep us in the Cup. We were all guilty of running about like headless chickens and I somehow found myself overlapping down the right flank and crossing for our centre-back Derek Mountfield to score.

I suspect Howard may have said he switched things and pulled off a masterstroke, but if that attack had broken down and they had gone up the other end and scored, we'd have had the bollocking to end all bollockings. It was pure luck and, at times like that, you think it's your year for the Cup. If the gaffer could have planned tactical stuff like that, he'd have been manager of Brazil, never mind Everton!

There was no time to recover and we were straight up to Ipswich for the replay which, again, proved to be another very difficult game. Howard told us that at this stage of competitions the team that makes the least mistakes gets the opportunity to progress, and they made one, conceding a penalty, with a needless hand ball. Sharp smashed it home and we were one game away from Wembley.

The semi-final was at Villa Park and we were, once again, hot favourites as we faced Luton who, like our previous opponents Ipswich, were fighting relegation. The game came after our mid-week trip to Munich, and I felt drained both physically and mentally.

Ricky Hill scored for Luton when we all felt Gary Stevens had been pushed in the build-up and, as hard as we tried, it seemed our luck wasn't in. But, as always, we kept plugging away and, with a minute or so to go, Kevin Sheedy scored from another long-range free kick. I would say it was not one of his greatest as it bounced a few times and just about hit the net, but the place went mental and I was just glad we had earned a draw.

I had never played in a semi-final and nobody had even discussed extra time, so when the final whistle went I was so happy that we had the chance of a rest and to play them again when we were not so tired. As I walked off, Big Nev shouted something like, 'Where are you going, soft lad?' I was then given the bad news that, despite hardly being able to walk, I had to do another 30 minutes! I was playing on pure adrenalin; I had never felt so exhausted in a game and I have no idea how I got through it. Villa Park was a nice stadium and central for most teams so an ideal neutral venue, but the pitch? It was never the best and the last thing you needed at that stage of the season, and after chasing Germans for 90 minutes solid a few days earlier, was 120 minutes running about on a mud patch with more sand covering the surface than grass. Still, a job needed doing and, from the first minute of extra time, I thought the Luton lads had it in their heads that they had blown their chance. To be a minute or so away from Wembley and to see it snatched away from you must have hurt them, and we were by far the better side for the remainder of the game.

As the minutes ticked away, all I was concentrating on was keeping things simple and getting the ball up to our forwards, as my father's request the day I signed at St Andrew's was playing my mind. All I could think of was, 'Don't make a mistake … and in a few weeks he could well be seeing me walk out at Wembley.'

With minutes to go, Sheedy swung another free kick into the box and Mountfield nearly burst the net with a bullet header and I went nuts! For the first time ever, I ran and joined in mobbing a goalscorer. As I have said, it was something I did not usually get involved in, but this time I could not hold back and it was a crazy couple of minutes, as we were joined by a couple of hundred fans in silly bobble hats chasing Mountfield around the pitch.

When the final whistle blew, I was elated; I had made it to my first ever Cup Final and knew that, as long as I could steer clear of injury and not get sent off before the big day in May, my dad's dream of seeing me walk out at Wembley would come true.

The Final on 18 May was a game too far for us and, although I was never one to moan about playing too many games, whichever clowns scheduled that fixture just three days after the Cup Winners' Cup Final needed their heads examining. It was a boiling hot day and we were not really at the races, and the jubilation we had enjoyed in Rotterdam turned to despair as United beat us 1–0 after extra time. Having beaten them a couple of times already that season – including the 5–0 hammering we gave them at Goodison – we were favourites to do the Treble, something never done by an English club, but it was just not to be. I still get grief in South Africa today from United and Liverpool fans about Whiteside's goal which turned out to be the one that won them the Cup. I think back to it most days and regret the build-up as when Norman picked the ball up, I cheekily said to him, 'Take me on ... run me!' I should have kept my mouth shut and just put him in the stands. Instead, I watched in horror as he dipped his shoulder and went inside me before curling in a shot that I would have expected Nev to save from that distance. Nev being Nev blamed himself, but I know deep down Norman should never have got that shot in, although to this day I think it was a cross. They held on and we were dejected and so upset to have not clinched our third cup of the season that day, as we were a better team than United. So although I had made my father's dream come true, I had a new one, as I was not happy just to have played at Wembley in an FA Cup Final – I wanted to win one.

I was fortunate enough to be given the chance just 12 months later as Everton reached their third FA Cup Final in as many seasons. After beating Exeter unconvincingly at home 1–0, thanks to a late Gary Stevens goal, we played Blackburn in a game when I scored for both teams in front of over 42,000 at Goodison. I can't remember my Everton strike for the life of me, but can remember the own-goal as I wanted the ground to open up and swallow me. A cross came from the right and one of their lads went for a header but completely missed the ball, which then hit me on the head and went into the right-hand corner of the goal past a shocked Nev. I was gutted and one look from big Nev was all I need to realise that we had better go on and win the game.

We did, but got a tough draw in the fifth round away to Spurs. The game was called off on the Saturday so we went to White Hart Lane mid-week and it was almost a mirror image of the game the season earlier when we as good as clinched the Championship there. Gary Stevens was out so Harper and Pointon lined up with myself and Rats in a makeshift back four, but Kevin went off injured early on which was a massive blow as I was the only recognised centre-half on the pitch as Inchy replaced him. We shuffled the pack and dug deep and Heath scored first before Lineker got a superb diving header to put us in control, but they nicked one late on and put us under some pressure, but we saw it out and were back in the quarters.

The draw was unkind and paired us with Luton on that wretched plastic pitch and was played just a couple of days after the Spurs win. Rats had not recovered, meaning I had to play alongside Alan Harper in the middle while Stevens and Pointon looked after the flanks. We played badly and were two down at one stage, but Howard shuffled things about and his tactical genius came up trumps. He pulled Pointon off for Inchy, we went three up top and hammered them for the remainder of the game. We got it back to two each and should have won it at the death but, considering the start we had given them, we were still glad to get them back to our place.

The replay at Goodison again saw myself and Harper in a under-strength back four but Luton had blown their chance on the Saturday and, once Lineker scored, we were never going to let them back in and we were one game away from Wembley again.

Another trip to Villa Park saw Sheffield Wednesday stand between us and a final against either Liverpool or Southampton and, once again, we were clear favourites, but Links was out and we lost Trevor Steven early on with a groin strain, which gave the Owls a great chance. Our strength in depth was fantastic and Harper came on and scored with a lob from about 20 yards, proving what a superb player he was for us. No matter where he played or what he was asked to do, he never let anyone down, a superb, versatile footballer without whom we would have needed another two or three squad players to do his job. They levelled when I think Mimms should have collected a ball swung into the six-yard box and, once again, we had to endure a further 30 minutes. This time it was Sharpy who scored with a classic volley to take us back to Wembley for the third year running.

The final against our Red neighbours can only be summed up as 'horrible'. It was a game we should have won having been one up and coasting after Lineker's 40th goal of the season. We had other chances, and they were falling out with each other, but we let them in with some sloppy passing and then Rush, as always, did us. It was so unlike us to concede goals like we did that day; collectively and individually we were poor.

We were comfortable when, from nothing, Gary Stevens gave the ball away and we were caught flat-footed as Rush rounded Mimms and it was all square. From coasting we were suddenly on the back foot and I remember the second goal with horror. As Molby got the ball in our box, I looked and I was marking both Dalglish and Craig Johnston. Jan hit it hard across the face of the goal and Kenny missed it, but it had too much pace for me, leaving Johnston to smash it in. We were all over the place. The third was worse; they broke, leaving us outnumbered, and the ball was played over my head to Rush who was unmarked and it was game over.

The season before was bad, but this was so much worse. We had handed Liverpool the Double in the space of two weeks and I was numb walking around the pitch at the end of the game. For some reason, the clubs had agreed to travel home together and that was a nightmare. Who in their right mind could organise such a stupid trip? I appreciate they wanted to promote the 'Merseyside United' theme, but I often wondered if the same thing would have gone ahead had we been the ones carrying the Cup? We got on the plane and they were sitting at the back with the trophy smiling like Cheshire Cats while we were all gutted at the front nursing hangovers. We had been treated to a superb party the night after the game as Howard had told us to go out and enjoy ourselves as we had put so much into the season.

I went to get in my seat but Barry Venison was in it and, at first, I politely asked him to move. I don't know if it was a wind-up or if he had genuinely sat in the wrong seat, but there was no reason for him to sit there so, when he didn't move, I said to him, 'I have asked you once, now get out of my seat before I fucking throw you out of it.' He quickly sulked off to join his team-mates at the back and that set the tone for the trip, and it was horrible having to follow them around the city centre as they had both cups and all we had was a few cases of beer.

The year before, we had lost the final but the tour of the city was superb as we celebrated the season's success and had the Championship trophy and Cup Winners' Cup to parade. This time we had nothing. I remember that we drank too much and were all dying for a piss so got the driver to stop and just ran to a house, knocked on the door and the lady and gentleman who owned it laughed as half the Everton team queued to use their toilet. Reidy was that pissed off that he refused to go on the tour and I wish I had done the same. Even the drink and the reception the Blues fans gave us could not lift my spirits; if I could change the result of any game I have played in, that would be the one.

The following season, I missed a third-round home victory over Southampton but was back for a win at Bradford when Snodds scored, and then again for the tough tie at Wimbledon in the fifth round. We went one up but were hammered 3–1 and I was taken off as the club missed out on making it a record four finals on the bounce. We were poor that day and had simply been out-fought by Wimbledon and it was disappointing as we knew we did not do ourselves justice and had let ourselves, the manager and the fans down.

The fifth round was again as far as we went a year later, but this time we had broken records getting that far. After mammoth games with Sheffield Wednesday, including three 1–1 draws and a 5–0 away win, we beat Middlesbrough after another three games before losing once again to Liverpool. It was a great Cup run; teams often win the fucker after just six games – we had played eight and not even made the quarter-finals.

The 1989 FA Cup Final was a sad occasion after the

142

Hillsborough tragedy; I'm glad to have played at Wembley that day, but often wonder if the game should have gone ahead given the circumstances.

In January that season, when the competition kicked off, we found ourselves losing at West Brom before Sheedy saved us with a late penalty and he scored again as we beat them in the replay. We came through another tricky game when we drew at Plymouth, but battered them in replay 4–0, giving us a trip to Barnsley in the fifth round. A week earlier, I'd picked up a knock and was ruled out for a few weeks and missed the game when an early Sharp goal took us through to the last eight. The three lower league teams had all given us a hard time but we came through and got an important home draw against Wimbledon and, although I missed the game again, I watched from the stands as we scraped through 1–0 thanks to a late Stuart McCall strike. Sharpy made a game of it when he missed a first-half penalty but, despite it being no classic, we were one game away from Wembley and, again, the dream was back on.

What can you say about the events of 15 April 1989? We beat Norwich in the semi-final thanks to a Pat Nevin goal, and were back at Wembley. There was no celebrating after the game and we were all shocked and saddened when we were told about the tragedy in Sheffield.

There was talk of the season being cancelled, but we went to Spurs on the Saturday after stopping off at Anfield in the week to pay our respects and it was an amazing sight to see so many tributes from fans all over the country. We then played Forest in the Simod Cup Final and my feelings on such competitions are well documented. We lost 4–3 and Wembley was half full – that tells you all you need to know about the worthless fixture.

Next up came Liverpool, who had decided to complete their fixtures. Before a full house at Goodison, the chairmen of both clubs led us out and it was very emotional night. The game ended goalless and it was very difficult match to play in.

We went into the Final on the back of three wins, including one at Old Trafford. I was fit, we were playing well and, despite Liverpool being favourites and the world wanting them to win, we were up for it and thought we could lift the Cup. Despite the sadness surrounding the event, we wanted to win it as much as ever; it was our job to go out and win it for the manager, for our fans and for ourselves.

Most neutrals were saying that it would be fitting if Liverpool won it for those who had lost their lives, but that did not come into it. If that was the case, the FA should have cancelled the competition that season and presented the Cup in memory of those who were killed. I would not have had a problem with that and, in fact, would have probably preferred it that way. But that option was not considered and, once the game was given the go-ahead, we were not just going to turn up and let Liverpool win.

The fairytale ending that the nation wanted was on the cards when Liverpool went ahead with an early John Aldridge goal and they held on until the last kick of the game when McCall scrambled one in for us. I was fully expecting it to be disallowed for offside, or for a foul or for anything. It would not have surprised me if, as it trickled in, the ref had blown his whistle and called full time before it hit the net, but he didn't and it was all square. There were fans all over the pitch and it was utter chaos as the reality that the goal had stood hit home. Once again, I thought that it was going to be our day.

I should have known better as soon as Rush came on for Aldo, as he did us again despite McCall scoring a fantastic second equaliser. Liverpool's winner gives me nightmares as I probably had the best view of it on the pitch. Barnes put a cross in and I thought it was ours to win all day, but somehow it landed between our two centre-backs and Rush just stooped and nodded it past Neville. It was a scandalous goal to concede and I knew that they would not let us back in for a third time, and I was right.

They saw out the remainder of the game and, when the final whistle blew, the pitch filled with fans and there were no laps of honour as things got bit out of hand. I had 'helped' a fan off the pitch when we had scored, but Bruce put one Liverpool fan on his arse as he tried to grab the Cup.

After the game, I thought it would be my last Cup Final and we had lost them all. If you have three goes at something, you would bet that one of them would come off and I will take to my grave the fact that I played in three FA Cup Finals for Everton and was not able to pick up just one winner's medal.

I did not know at the time but that was to be my last game for Everton. I had started my Everton career with a defeat in London and ended it with one, I know which defeat hurt the most. I would have swapped our second League Championship to have won the Cup that day. I really wanted to do that for Everton but, sadly, some things are just not meant to be.

12

ALL CHANGE

After regaining the Championship and, once again, happy that it was business as usual, the bombshell news landed that Howard had resigned and gone to manage in Spain. I was shell-shocked. Had he gone a year earlier after missing out on the League and Cup in a week to Liverpool, and having sold Lineker to Barcelona, I would probably have understood it a bit more. We were champions, had a decent squad and, in all honesty, Athletic Bilbao were hardly Real Madrid or Barcelona, so I could not understand it. And as it all happened during pre-season, there were no goodbyes – he was just gone.

Maybe Howard thought he had taken us as far as he could, given that the European ban had kicked in. Maybe he just fancied a change. Either way, it was a sad day for

Everton Football Club. One positive thing to come out of it all was that Colin Harvey had agreed to stay and take over from Howard, at least meaning that we avoided bringing in some outsider with no idea how the club worked.

All the lads respected Colin; he was a great coach and I don't think there was a single player unhappy when he was appointed to replace Howard. The only difference for us was having to call him 'boss', not Colin. He never asked for that, it was mutual respect from the players, but it was something that he never really seemed comfortable with.

His first season in charge was always going to be tough and, even though we got off to a good start when we won the Charity Shield beating Coventry at Wembley, we hardly got going in the league and never looked like we were ever in with a chance of retaining the Championship. To make the season even more depressing, Liverpool had an unbelievable campaign, going unbeaten from their opening game right through to the end of March when they equalled Leeds United's record for the longest unbeaten run in league history from the start of a season. It was nice to beat them to stop them overtaking Leeds' record but, in fairness, they won the league at a canter. Although we finished fourth, it was a poor season by our previous standards, made even worse by the fact they also knocked us out of the FA Cup.

We beat them in the League Cup at Anfield, as well as the game at Goodison, but the problem was nobody else could and they only lost a further two games all season. Once again, our home form was decent – we only lost two games at Goodison – but we won just five games away from home which was diabolical, considering we were reigning champions.

We came close to making it to Wembley again, but lost in the League Cup semis to Arsenal and, without blaming the amount of injuries we had, we rarely had a settled side. If I can put my finger on one thing that hindered us more than anything it was Kevin Ratcliffe missing half the season and, although I did OK at centre-back, quite simply we were not the same side without him in it.

Once again, the FA threw some stupid games our way to compensate for the lack of European football and we ended up playing in one of the craziest tournaments ever organised, as about a dozen clubs played a mini knock-out competition staged over two days at Wembley. What a waste of time and money! Mickey Mouse competitions like the Mercantile Credit Football League Centenary Trophy could not replace the revenue or the importance of European football. I just wish that the people who had decided to deprive us of the opportunity of playing in either the European or UEFA Cup had the balls to admit that we did not deserve to be banned. We had done no wrong and we should have been allowed back in, but those responsible for the decisions were people in high places who don't ever admit it when they get things wrong. Hence we were given worthless games to play and not the competitive European football we had earned and deserved.

We flew to one such tournament in Dubai in December for an unofficial British Championship game against Rangers. I never played but, while we were over there, a group of players were sitting around the bar when Gary Stevens introduced me to an air hostess he knew. I went over and she asked me to kiss her. I did, whereupon she got hold of my hand and I made the walk of shame past the lads, took her to my room and did the business. I must have been on top form as this girl was obviously no virgin, and later told Gary that I was red-hot in the sack. I was well happy! What he never knew was when we were at it, I fell off the bed and aggravated my hamstring injury and probably missed a couple more games thanks to focussing on my libido rather than my fitness!

It was a poor first season, not just for Colin but for us all, endorsed by the fact that my personal highlights were a top shag in Dubai and preventing Liverpool getting a record, which is sad really. I was beginning to think it was no longer business as usual.

Things were beginning to go a bit flat and there was plenty of talk of players moving on but, in pre-season, only Gary Stevens and Derek Mountfield were sold. I was especially sad to see Gary leave as, from day one at the club, he was my room partner and we had some superb times together. Colin brought in Neil McDonald to replace Gary, Pat Nevin from Chelsea and Stuart McCall, all for good money, but the signing that excited everyone was when Tony Cottee chose us before Arsenal for a British record fee. They were all big signings so the board had certainly backed Colin and it looked like we were going to have a real go at getting the title back.

Unfortunately, it was at this time that I had arrived back

from the Welsh tour in some discomfort and went to see the doctor at Everton at once as things were not looking good. As well as my privates being a bit sore, my ankle was in a bad way, although I thought it was a totally different issue and had no idea it was connected.

As soon as the doc saw me he sent me to a private hospital the club used and they diagnosed me with NSU – non-specific urethritis – a sexually-transmitted disease which causes inflammation of the urethra. I had all the classic symptoms of an old-fashioned dose, the pain and burning sensation when I had a piss, a bit of cloudy discharge and a feeling that I needed to pass urine frequently ... but I had no idea how this affected my ankle.

As I was diagnosed with a common STD, they carried out a few more tests and I had to stay in overnight, awaiting the results. The following morning, I could not stand up, could put no weight whatsoever on my ankle and was absolutely shitting myself. They told me that whatever this slapper in Malta had passed on to me, it had got into my blood and found its way to my ankle and that the inflammation caused by the STD could have ended my career.

It was that serious that if I had left it for another week and I could have been finished. Luckily, I was not stupid enough to have hoped it would go away by itself, and the early diagnosis and immediate treatment helped me carry on as a footballer, albeit not a very professional one.

I spent nearly a month in hospital and the club, never mind Mrs Van Den Hauwe, were none too impressed. There were all sorts of rumours going about that I had been stabbed, was a smack-head, or had had my leg broken by gangsters ... but the fact was I had a dose, a very bad one. A nurse called Karen was given the job of looking after me and it was a little embarrassing as she knew exactly why I was there and it was not because my ankle was a bit swollen. It did not help that she was also a very good-looking young lady!

As the weeks went by, we got quite close and, one night, she sneaked me out of the hospital to a pub owned by a former Everton winger, Gary Jones. By now she assured me that I was OK to have a drink as I was off the medication and just rehabilitating, so there I was, sitting on a bar stool with my leg all strapped up, drinking with a tasty nurse whom the club were paying to look after me! With not drinking for weeks, I was soon pissed and ended up falling off the bar stool, so Nurse Karen got me out of there having decided to look after me *really* well. She gave me the good news that the dose had gone and then took me back to her place and sorted me out in every way imaginable. The following morning, she managed to sneak me back into the hospital before I was missed which was good for the both of us, for if the club would have found out, we'd have been sacked. That's how far out of control I was; basically, I didn't give a fuck, and that makes me feel ashamed looking back but, at the time, that's how it was.

So through my own stupidity, I missed the start of the season. It felt like I was jinxed but, of course, I wasn't – I just wasn't taking enough care of myself off the pitch. Although we hammered Newcastle 4–0 when Cottee scored a hat-trick on his début and then won at Coventry, a draw at home to Forest and then three defeats on the bounce to Millwall, Luton and Wimbledon saw us dropping well into the bottom half of the table before I was fit to start my season.

I began to think that the lads Colin had brought in were not as good as those they had replaced. In all due respect to Neil McDonald, he was not an England international like Gary Stevens and, although Cottee seemed to get plenty of goals, was he an Everton player? Yes, he scored goals, but was he doing enough outside the opponent's box? Tony was a lovely guy and, due to my London connections, I also became friends with his father, but I never felt he was truly at home at Goodison. Pat Nevin was an odd bod, a tricky winger, but was no Kevin Sheedy and, as much as I admired Stuart McCall, who worked his bollocks off every game, he quite simply did not have anywhere near as much class as Paul Bracewell.

Although my ankle had cleared up, the blood disorder took its toll on my general fitness and I could not get fully fit and play enough games to nail down a position in the side, despite the fact we were hardly setting the league on fire. Inchy and Peter Reid were shipped out and the press were forever linking Trevor Steven with a move to Rangers, so it looked like 'the boys of '85' were no more – and, sadly, that proved to be the case.

Despite our run in the FA Cup and a silly appearance at Wembley in yet another half-hearted competition called the Simod Cup – invented once again to fill in for missing out on European football – it was a season I'd rather forget. We ended up finishing eighth in the league and, deep down, I knew that it was time to move on. It was not just a football decision but, off the pitch, I was getting deeper and deeper in trouble and, for the sake of Susan and my gorgeous baby daughter Gemma, I felt my time at Everton was up.

I was sitting at home one day during pre-season and Sharpy popped round and said Gary Lineker had been on the phone to him and had asked him whether I was now fully fit. He said that Links had asked me to give him a call, so I did, and he said Terry Venables was interested in signing me and would I consider speaking to him? I suppose in a way it's an illegal approach, but that's how it worked. We were all guilty of it and, if ever your club wanted to sign a player, there were always ways and means of getting to him. In this case, it was via Links and Sharpy and I think Graeme was hoping I'd bugger off due to the amount of scraps I was getting him involved in every time we went for a pint!

The way I saw it, I had nothing to lose, so I told Mr Venables to go about his business through the proper channels and I'd see what Colin said when Everton were formally approached. Deep down, I knew I'd go; as I saw it, the team was breaking up, I was forever in the shit on Merseyside and needed to get the fuck out of there before my marriage disintegrated as quickly as our Championship side was doing.

Within a few days, Colin called me in and said Tottenham Hotspur had come in for me and that they had made an offer acceptable to the board of directors and did I want to go? I told him I did, and he asked me my reasons. I told him it was nothing to do with him taking over from Howard but, for the sake of my family, I really needed to get away from Merseyside. Out of the blue, he told me he wanted me to stay and offered me a new four-year deal that included a decent raise at the start of every season which was far better than what was on offer at Spurs. The boss also said he wanted me to move into the centre of defence, a position I had always felt more comfortable in, but my mind was made up – I declined Colin's more-than-generous offer.

As much as I respected him, appreciated his offer and, as much as I loved Everton Football Club, I told Colin that I wanted to join Spurs. He seemed genuinely disappointed but wished me well. He was a lovely man and, given the fact I had caused him no end of problems with my off-the-field antics, it was a credit to him that he did not just tell me to empty my locker and piss off.

In those days, very few players had agents, so I flew down to London, met Mr Venables and agreed with everything he put on the table. There was no signing-on fee, no extra dough; in fact, it probably cost me money to join Spurs, but deep down I had to go and signed with a heavy heart. I never met any of the Everton lads to say my goodbyes – I was not that kind of person – and combined with the fact that I was sad to leave, it hit me hard.

Looking back now, it was a bit naughty the way the move came about and, yes, I do regret it, but Spurs were building a top side. The likes of Lineker and Gascoigne were huge names at the time so it was a new start for me. I never really saw it as a dream move like the one to Everton, but neither did I see it as the nightmare it was about to become.

13

WINNING – AND LOSING – MY SPURS

Terry Venables was probably one of the few managers who could have convinced me to leave Everton. He was so well-respected in the game – he still is – and even today is still the people's choice every time the England job becomes available. That is the measure of the man and his skills as a coach.

When we spoke about the move, he told me that, in his opinion, Tottenham were just a couple of players short from having a team capable of challenging for honours and he saw me as one of those required to take Spurs to the next level. I was in awe of his mannerisms and the way he conducted himself during our meeting, Terry oozed class and he talked the talk, but was more than capable of walking the walk as well. He had been back at Spurs for a couple of seasons and had built a good side with the likes of Gary Lineker and Paul Gascoigne, world-class players who would walk into any top side. The fact that he believed I could help him win something made the move seem a fantastic opportunity, particularly as things at Everton had apparently gone stale.

The move was finalised and I signed for Tottenham Hotspur on 25 August 1989 for £575,000 and the deal was completed on the night of my new club's game – at Everton! I did not go to the match but listened to it on the radio as my old team-mates ran out 2–1 winners. Who I was supporting that night I can't say!

I made my début in a 2–0 defeat at Aston Villa, played OK and kept my place for the next game, when we were well and truly dicked 4–1 at home by Chelsea. It was a home début from hell and my one memory is watching a long ball go down the middle and thinking it was safe as houses, Kerry Dixon latching on to it before chipping our 'keeper from outside the area. I realised in that split-second that Thorstvedt was no Southall.

We beat Southend 1–0 for my first win bonus but we were not playing well as a side. Then we suddenly clicked and, despite losing the second leg to Southend who took us to extra time before we went though on the away goals rule, we won four league games on the bounce before thrashing Manchester United 3–0 in the League Cup at Old Trafford. Things were looking good, although the results against Southend and United were typical of how inconsistent we could be. We were capable of beating anyone when we played well, but the problem was we were capable of being beaten by anyone when we played not so well. We were either very good or shit – we were never average.

Off the pitch, I had a bit of luck when my old mate from Liverpool, Dave Dolby, got in touch and told me he had moved to London and had a boozer I might like to visit. What a place it turned out to be, as it was situated right opposite a huge dance college called the Italia Conti Dancing School. After one visit to the pub, I was hooked and, once training was out of the way, I would go there as every day the place would be full of these beautiful dance students. I was in heaven!

One night, I ended up in bed with a pair of young ladies from the dance school and they were absolute stunners – one was from Coventry, the other a London girl. Eventually, after giving them both a bit of a tickle, the local girl left us to it and I had a great time with the one from Coventry. I had some of the best times of my Spurs career in that pub and, to this day, I can't understand why I never opted for the dancing girls instead of Mandy. One setback was that I got hooked on the Guinness, and it only took a few weeks before Mr Venables noticed I had put a few pounds on and told me quite clearly to get off the stuff.

The first thing I noticed when I began to drink in central London was that everyone was walking about with these brick-sized mobile phones. They were not for me and, although I was given one by the club, probably to keep me on their radar, I was forever losing it and leaving it lying around. Eventually, I smashed it against the wall and never bothered with phones again until they became much smaller.

After just a couple of months, money was slipping through my fingers like water. I was on a good contract at Spurs but almost everything in London was twice the price as it was in Liverpool, and I was forever going to the club for a cash advance. Every week, I'd be borrowing from my monthly salary until one month there was nothing left to pay the bills. My missus rang the club and asked them what the hell was going on and, a day later when I went for a sub, the lady in the office in charge of the petty cash said she was sorry but Mr Venables had told her that I was not to have any more money from her and that was that. I tried a few times as you do, but Terry's word was final and I got nothing again until payday.

I thought a move from Merseyside would calm me down but things just carried on as normal once I found a few pubs to my liking, and I went missing for the first time at Spurs over the Christmas period and missed the game against Millwall. I turned up at the lads' Christmas party the following day and some were not too happy with me. I also had a right old boot in tow with me, so I ditched her and got on with the party and already my attitude was fuck 'em all!

I went into training the following day after calling home to make my peace with Susan, who by now was used to it. I was not doing it every week, but every so often I needed a blow out and just went missing for a few days. It sounds mad now, but at the time it was all just routine for me.

Terry got me in the office and was rightly not happy with me; he knew my every move and, as Howard had at Everton, also had some great spies in the camp. He never bollocked me as such, he was so calm, but told me plainly and simply that I had let everyone down. There was no ranting and raving but, by the time I got out of his office, I felt like I had been battered around the room with a baseball bat by him. The simple things he told me were worse than a punch, a kick or any verbal bashing. He was an absolute master when it came to letting you know right from wrong and, from that day on, I tried my utmost to never let him down again.

Despite going AWOL, I was back in the side for the following game against Nottingham Forest and Paul Walsh had a moan in the papers about my return while he was keeping the bench warm. We sat down after training and I told Walshy straight, 'Since when have you been a left-back, you prick?' Terry intervened and told Walsh that he picked the team and that he was not going to cut his nose off to spite his face, adding that I was the best left-back Spurs had available and that I was playing – end of!

After the game, my friend Tommy Hayes gave me a lift into town to meet my top adviser Nick Trainer and, as he was a well-to-do solicitor, he was always immaculately dressed. The only problem was that he had the worst taste in ties you have ever seen. We were in a wine bar with the gorgeous lady who ran it and were enjoying a lovely drink and chat when I said to Nick that he should remove his tie. He laughed at my suggestion so I went into kitchen area and picked up this huge chopping knife which was the size of a machete and slipped it down my sock.

We carried on laughing about his tie with me telling him I was that pissed off with it that it was time to remove it, but again he refused. We ended up leaving and, as we walked down the road, I grabbed his precious neck accessory, pulled the knife out, raised it above my head and chopped the tie off in one slice, missing his nose by half an inch!

People in the street were running about thinking we were having a serious set-to and the lady from the bar could not believe what she had just witnessed. She managed to get the knife off me and back in the kitchen before somebody called the police and I found myself locked up. We stayed on the piss all night with Nick still wearing the knot of his tie as the stubborn bugger still refused to take it off. I ended up with the bar manager and had a great night. That was one of the first and only times I have ever seen Mr Nick Trainer speechless!

Back on the pitch, I played the majority of games that season, missing the odd one with injury or suspension, but was first choice unless rested for the League Cup when Terry decided to give a few squad players a run out. After beating United, we fancied our chances but were knocked out by Forest after a replay, despite coming back from their place with a draw. And as for the FA Cup, well, it was the usual disaster as I missed the third-round game at home to Southampton when we were dumped out 3–1.

Our League form improved immensely and I played in a 2–1 win against my mates Everton, eventually winning eight of our last ten league games to finish third, a position today that would guarantee Champions League football. It was a great effort, although we lost 13 games, 9 were by the odd goal. That really was a season when I look back at it and think we were probably just a couple of quality players or a few clean sheets away from being a team that could have been champions. The Champions League today is what everyone aims for, but then it did not have the same rewards, so we looked upon it as progression, not success. I was really looking forward to the new season, for the way we had finished the previous one and with a full pre-season behind me, I thought we would be in with a great chance of challenging for the title.

Spurs got off to a great start as we beat Manchester City 3–1 and went 13 games unbeaten and were flying before we lost at Liverpool. I was playing every week and loving my football again. As was the case the previous year, Terry rested me for League Cup games playing Justin Edinburgh in my place, which was no problem, but I badly wanted to be back in for fifth-round tie with Chelsea. I'll never know if I'd have been selected as I was injured for the game which we lost 3–0 in a replay at White Hart Lane, having done what we thought was the hard part when we drew at their place. The Wembley jinx was happening at Spurs as it had at Goodison but, to make things worse, our League form was abysmal for the second half of the season, too.

After the Liverpool defeat, we went another four games unbeaten, so had lost just once in eighteen games, including a 1–1 draw against Everton on my return to Goodison,

163

when I received a fantastic reception from the Goodison faithful. We then won just another three games in the League all season and finished a disappointing tenth. I played almost every game and, despite the dreadful run and woeful league position, my dream of winning the FA Cup came true when, on 18 May, Tottenham beat Nottingham Forest 2–1 at Wembley to ease the heartache of my three Cup Final defeats there with Everton.

We made hard work of it getting to the semi-finals, even though the draw was kind to us. I sat out a 1-0 win at Blackpool, but played every game after as we eased past Oxford at home before going to Portsmouth for the fifth-round tie. I will always remember this game as I played a great ball through to Gascoigne, which he tucked away to set up a quarter-final against Notts County which we nicked 2–1. After the Pompey game, Gazza said the ball through to him was one of the best he had ever received and I was truly thrilled. A week later, he said exactly the same thing to Vinny Samways and the following week to Walshy, and I began to think mine hadn't really been that special.

The semi at Wembley against Arsenal was a bit like the one I had played for Everton against Bayern Munich, insomuch as after such a fantastic win, the final was always going to be an anti-climax. The goal Gazza scored from a free kick that day is up there with the best strikes I have had the good fortune to witness and it set us up nicely for a 3–1 win against our closest rivals. Lineker got the other two goals and the joy in the dressing room after the game was as good as it gets, but Terry had to remind the lads that you win nothing for being victorious in a semi-final. I was one player he did not need to mention that to.

As a senior player, I must take some responsibility for not getting a grip of Gazza on the day of the Final and trying to calm him down. From the minute we had breakfast, he was like a man possessed and I am amazed he made it to Wembley for the game as he was that wound up. As it was, we let Gazza be Gazza and he ended up making that crazy tackle after just a few minutes and his Cup dreams were in tatters as he was stretchered off and taken to hospital.

Without Paul and with the circumstances that surrounded his exit, the game was somewhat subdued but we won it 2–1 thanks to a Paul Stewart strike and an own-goal from Forest legend Des Walker. Lineker was relieved as he had earlier missed a penalty that could have won us the game and, when the final whistle blew, despite feeling a bit sorry for Des, I was just glad that my Cup jinx was over and I was a proud man climbing the steps to collect my winner's medal.

The record books show that, two days after the Cup Final, I missed our final league game at Manchester United and, to this day, I have no idea why. If I did go missing, I'm sure Terry wasn't too bothered as the Cup was back in the Spurs trophy room.

After the Cup Final, we were told the extent of Gazza's injury and asked Terry if we could take the Cup and his medal to the hospital. He agreed and off we went, straight to Gazza's ward, and found him putting on a brave face in front of a gang of nurses. As soon as we walked in, he was so emotional – he cried, as usual – but was genuinely touched by our gesture but it was the least we could do. I had won an FA Cup Final at Wembley on my fourth attempt, so knew what Cup Final heartache was all about. Although Paul had a winner's medal at his first attempt, it probably didn't mean much as the injury and the fact it would balls up his move to Lazio probably overshadowed the victory for him.

Gazza was a great lad and such good fun to be with. We were out one Christmas with the lads and Gazza was in tow and, as usual, 100 per cent nuts. We were walking down the street and he noticed a tramp sleeping in a doorway with a pile of cardboard boxes covering him to keep the poor bugger warm. Gazza took a massive run and did one of those high-jump leaps and landed bang in the middle of the boxes while this poor tramp was almost crushed to death. I thought it was a bit out of order, to be honest; the old fella was wheezing and could not get his breath, but Gazza thought it was hilarious and was pissing himself. He eventually checked the tramp was OK before we walked off to another bar after giving him a £50 note for his troubles. The man was as mad a March hare, totally crazy – lovely, but crackers.

He was also guilty of having too many hangers-on in his company, something we all warned him about, but he had a heart of gold and saw the good in everyone despite the fact that they were like leeches on him. I wonder where those leeches are today when I believe he is really in need of true friends to help him through a difficult time in his life.

Am I shocked to see him the way he is? If I'm honest, no, as he did everything to the extreme. I am, however, sad to see such a fantastic footballer and quality person suffering as he is, and truly wish him all the best in his recovery.

He did take the pressure off me from time to time, and I remember one morning when we were all in training and Terry said that Gazza would be in a bit late as he had been home for the weekend and the train he was on to London was running late. In true Gazza style, he turned up about two hours later, pissed as a fart, as he'd drunk the train dry. We all looked at him and he had that cheeky grin of his and we could tell he was steaming. Terry knew but did not bollock him; he just told him to do his running and then had a little word in his ear. Once again, it was quality man-management, as the next day Paul was first in and worked his bollocks off.

After the Cup win, instead of building on that success, the club's fortunes went into freefall as Terry moved upstairs after a failed bid to buy the club. I know nothing about the politics that went on, but have been told that Terry failed in a £20m bid to take over Spurs with a bloke called Larry Gillick, having been outbid by Alan Sugar. For whatever reason, Terry was then was appointed Chief Executive by Sugar and Pete Shreeves was appointed as our new gaffer.

Anyone in their right mind could see that the change was a backward step, and the players and the fans were rightly pissed off, but Sugar was in total control and, if we liked him or not, it made no difference – what Sugar wanted, Sugar got. In his own mind, he obviously thought he was bigger than the club and that is not healthy, as he managed to cause so much unrest there nobody benefited.

On the training ground, Terry was a superb coach. There were very few in the world better than him; we hardly ever saw him as Doug and Clem would supervise the sessions, but Terry would walk over and watch us for 20 minutes then pull us together to point out a few minor things we were doing wrong – at set pieces, for example – and he would always be right. His attention to the finer details could not be bettered.

Shreeves was a decent fella but no Terry Venables. His training was a bit happy-tappy and I never really enjoyed it and, obviously, his methods never worked as on the pitch things went from bad to worse and he was sacked after just one season.

The campaign of decline began back at Wembley as we drew with Arsenal to get a six-month share of the Charity Shield. I was headline news in the papers after a couple of minor issues, one a good, old-fashioned, crunching tackle on Lee Dixon, who reacted like he'd been shot with a cannon ball, and the other a stray arm that I landed on David Rocastle. I suppose I could have had a yellow for both and had the embarrassment of being sent off at Wembley, but it was only a friendly and the referee, a Mr Terry Holbrook, showed common sense, something sadly lacking in today's game, and gave me one yellow and a good bollocking.

Dixon and Rocastle were different in their views of the incidents. Whereas the full-back had a pop and made a fuss,

Rocky got on with it and later gave me a kick back, which earned him a yellow card, too. After the game, we shook hands and had a good laugh about it over a beer. David was a top bloke and excellent player, and I was very sad to hear that he had passed away aged only 33 just a couple of months after he announced that he was suffering from non-Hodgkin's lymphoma, an aggressive form of cancer which attacks the immune system.

Personally, the season was a nightmare for me as I picked up a knock in a shock 1–0 loss at Swansea early in the season and missed four games before I was back in the side which then went on a dreadful run. I eventually lost my place to Justin Edinburgh after a dicking at Leeds, but played a few games at right-back alongside him. Even at that stage of my Spurs career, I began to think that the writing was on the wall for me and, looking back, it probably was, as I never fully established myself in the side again.

It was a season to forget, despite reaching the European Cup Winners' Cup quarter-finals, where we were knocked out at Feyenoord in a game marred by crowd trouble. Gary Lineker scored 28 league goals in his final season for the club, but we suffered 20 defeats and finished 15th in the First Division, which was simply not good enough for Sugar and Shreeves was axed.

I was not sorry to see him go; I had no grudge with him but wanted to be playing more football and he obviously fancied Edinburgh at left-back, so froze me out. With Shreeves gone, I thought I'd have a better chance of regaining my place. I was glad I never put good money on it!

Most of the lads, myself included, were hoping for a big-name appointment or, better still, Terry giving up his executive role and getting back to what he did best, but we got neither as Doug Livermore and Ray Clemence were appointed as joint managers for the inaugural season of the newly formed Premier League.

Once it was confirmed that Ray and Dougie were to take over first-team affairs, I decided from the off to get myself 100 per cent fit and give it my best shot at winning back a regular place in the side. What a waste of time that was! I trained harder than I had ever done and even agreed without a moan to play out of position on the left side of midfield to show the joint bosses that I was up for a challenge, but no matter how hard I tried or how well I played, I once again found myself being frozen out. If I'm honest, I was disappointed with Dougie and Clem as I had had no previous beef with them, but even when I politely asked them about my continual absence from the side, they would not give me any answers.

I accepted that I was not their first-choice left-back, but stuck with the training and did not go knocking on doors asking for a move when maybe I should have. After a few games, Edinburgh was injured and I played six games and did reasonably well, but was dropped as soon as Justin regained fitness. I then filled in at right-back and again did no better or worse than anyone else, but then missed over 20 games apart from a couple of substitute appearances,

Left: Millwall. No-one likes us we don't care!

Below: With Ray Parr, owner of the superb No9 House on Goodison Road.

Above: Myself and John with one South African player I wish I'd had on my books!

Below: The Gaffer! Howard Kendall.

Above: Myself, Andy Nicholls, Sandy Brown and Colin Harvey.

Below: With Terry Venables and my beautiful daughter Gemma.

Above: Little Nobby, an East End legend.

Below: A true gentleman, Big Frank Bruno.

Above: A guest at Gary Jones' wedding. I had some fantastic times when Gary ran The Albert on Lark Lane.

Below: At Joey Junior's 40th.

Above: Another night in The Conti with Joey Senior and the lads.

Below: The legendary Conti. With Joey Bennett Junior.

Above: Looking a bit nervous before one of my first after dinner talks at Alan Stubbs' bar in Birkdale.

Below: With Franny and Cocky after a great night on the Wirral. The fans' reception at such nights truly touched me.

Above: With my agent Andy at the Boys of 85 reunion. An amazing night.

Below: At home in Cape Town with my wife Carolyn and close friends John and Lynne Smith.

including one at my beloved Goodison Park when Spurs beat Everton 2–1. It was a terrible game and I was a sad figure sitting on the bench. Goodison was dead. There were less than 20,000 in the ground and, although the fans once again gave me a great reception, I could not help but think that the glory days were gone and Everton were another club in decline. That saddened me more than my own plight at Spurs, as Everton were a superb club and to see them struggling in a ground less than half full was very sad.

I can remember coming on as a sub to play alongside Ruddock and him shouting to the opposition forwards that they were fucked now as there was no way they would score past us two. I think he enjoyed playing alongside me, as we were similar types of players and similar characters off the pitch.

Once again, Edinburgh picked up a knock so I made my comeback at Bramall Lane and we got hammered 6–0 by Sheffield United, and it must have been my entire fault as I was back out of the side for the following game. I played in the last four games of the season, including another 6–1 lashing at Anfield, but did a lot better when we beat Arsenal on the last game of the season to give us a top-ten finish and the title of top dogs in North London, albeit in the league only, as the Gunners went on to win the Cup a week later, so I doubt they were too concerned with that reverse.

Arsenal got to the Final having beaten us in the semi-final at Wembley a few weeks earlier. I had played in the game a week prior to the big Cup-tie – a 3–1 win against Manchester City – and was devastated not to keep my place for the

Wembley showdown. I lost my rag and asked Clem straight out whether he and Doug had a problem with me. All I got back was bullshit about keeping my chin up and training hard. It was bollocks – I had done that all season and it was simply that somebody had marked my card. Clemence and Livermore were weak in my eyes; if they did have a problem with me, why not just come clean? If they didn't think I was good enough, then sell me. All they did was give me excuse after excuse as to why I was not in the team, and that had a significantly adverse affect on my career and life in general as, once again, I hit the booze and started to fuck my life up again.

I thought my time at Spurs was up but, out of the blue, Terry and the lads were sacked and the chairman appointed none other than Ozzie Ardiles as manager. I was gutted to see Terry leave his beloved Spurs due to internal feuds and a clash of personalities with Sugar, but did not think that the appointment of Ardiles would mean I would soon be joining him out of the door.

Ardiles was a strange choice as manager, as he had no top-flight pedigree, having previously managed Swindon, Newcastle and West Bromwich Albion, all in the lower leagues and all without winning anything other than the odd play-off final. It had been over ten years since I had last met him and I never gave it a second thought when we were summoned one by one to Ozzie's office for a private face-to-face meeting with the new gaffer.

I walked in, shook his hand and sat down, and immediately noticed that the chair he was in was too big for him. He looked like a little kid sitting behind the desk and, as I began to introduce myself, he said, 'I know who you are … you kicked me once at Birmingham and insulted me and my country!' I was gobsmacked, and then he showed me this small scar on his leg and carried on saying I could have ended his career. I sensed it was payback time and got the impression he was hell-bent on ending mine as he said he had made his mind up that Justin Edinburgh was going to be his number-one left-back. He went on to say that if I was to stay at the club, I would have to prove myself to him in training that I was good enough to feature in his squad.

I asked him bluntly whether it was a personal thing, and he just kept repeating that I needed to prove myself to him. Prove what, for fuck's sake? Was he saying that everything I had achieved in my career meant nothing, because I had done him when I was a raw teenager at Birmingham? The bloke was an out-and-out bastard; I would have had far more respect for him had he said 'I don't like you' and that I should look elsewhere, but he never had the balls to say that.

As soon as training began, I realised the extent of the situation I was in. We were split into two groups – first team and reserves – and told by the coaches what the sessions involved. Andy Gray and myself were then told to do our own thing, so we would just run round the pitch for an hour and piss off home. We just turned up every day and did nothing. After a few weeks, I confronted Ardiles in his office and asked him straight if there was any chance of me playing for him or should I move on. He told me that my chances of making the reserves, let alone the first team, were slim and that he would listen to offers for me. I thought, that's OK, and left.

The following day I was told that Norwich had enquired about my availability but were informed I was not available, so I went and knocked on Ardiles' door again and asked him why I wasn't available for a transfer when a day earlier he had told me I was? Basically, he said that I could not join another Premiership club.

By now, I was beginning to lose my rag, so made the point of going to see him every day to enquire if anyone had made an offer for me. Ozzie was soon sick of the sight of me, at the same time each day – Knock, knock ... 'Hello, any news?' ... 'No, sorry, go and run around the park with Andy Gray!'

He soon got sick of me knocking on his door, so he foolishly told his assistant that if I went to his office again, they should say he was out. I knew he was lying, so I booted his door open, I almost took it off its hinges and he shit himself! I was totally gone and told him to stop treating me like a child and warned him to get me a move or he was going through the window. One wrong word from him and I'd have given him a proper hiding there and then.

Mick McCarthy phoned me the next day and said that they had enquired about my availability, and Ardiles had simply told him to get in touch as he wanted nothing to do with me, hence giving me the green light to speak to Millwall. That day, I walked out on Spurs a happy man. I was sad to leave the club and the supporters, but just thrilled that I never had to set eyes on that horrible little man Ardiles ever again.

There were a few issues to sort out when Ozzie did his best to fuck the move up but I eventually signed at Millwall on the day my old team-mates went up to Anfield and came back with a massive three points after winning 2–1. For a few days, I wondered if I had left too quickly and was Ardiles the man to bring the good times back to Spurs? My fears were ungrounded, as it turned out – he did nothing to improve the team or the club in general. While I am not a person to wish ill to others, I was truly delighted that Ardiles lost his job the following season as I had no respect whatsoever for the man, and feel no differently about him today.

14

FATAL ATTRACTION

I left Everton for a number of reasons, one of which was to save my marriage, as the life I was leading in Liverpool was driving a huge wedge between Susan and myself. We bought a big house in Chislehurst, Kent, that cost me £175,000. It is now valued at over £1 million. Once fully furnished, it was a superb place to live but, soon after moving in, I started going out with a bloke called Harold. He was an uncle to Paul Walsh who, in turn, was married to Mandy Smith's cousin. Harold was a man about town and he introduced me to some nice bars and pubs and, one day, we were having a drink in his favourite wine bar when Paul Walsh said they had arranged a surprise for me.

I was never one for surprises, so was a bit nervy when, half-an-hour later, a young lady named Amanda Louise

Smith, the daughter of local snooker hall manager Robert John Smith, walked into the bar and into my life, with her mother Patsy. Knowing what I know now, I would have jumped out of the window before we even said hello. I never had a clue who she was, but could not help notice she was a stunning-looking girl.

We hit it off at once and she asked me to dance. As much as I wanted to, I just couldn't throw myself on to an empty dance floor and have a jig with her as I would have looked a proper mug. I thought it was a set-up by the lads and politely declined, which saw them say their goodbyes and leave. I don't think she liked the fact that I wouldn't dance with her, even though deep down I wanted to. That should have made me realise she was someone who wanted her own way, or would become quite moody if she didn't get what she wanted, and I regret not sussing that out on that fateful first meeting.

I thought that was the end of it, but Walshy told me in training that Mandy fancied me and was really disappointed that I would not dance with her. He set it up for me and Harold to call in on them at home one night, which we did. It became a regular pastime as we would just pop in and have a chat and a drink with them all; it was nothing serious, we were just enjoying each other's company.

By now Walshy had told me about Mandy's failed relationship with Bill Wyman and it was a horror story. It has been well documented in no end of tabloids and glossy magazines that Wyman started dating Mandy when she was just 13, and how she blamed him for her poor state of mind.

My take on it is simple and to the point – if a normal man on the street would have become involved with a 13-year-old girl when he was about 40, he would not be adored by the British public.

I got close to Mandy, we talked for hours and I really felt sorry for her. She had an eating disorder and was forever being sick; it was truly sad. At this time, her mother was superb with me; she blamed everything on Wyman, yet where had she been when he was apparently sleeping with her? Under the same roof but, no doubt, turning a blind eye to the situation. They say love is blind; no doubt wanting fame and fortune at any cost is also blind.

One night I was asked by her mother – who, by now, I had realised, controlled everything Mandy did – whether I'd like to stop over as Mandy felt so low. I agreed and slept on the floor next to Mandy's bed and held her hand all night; it was extremely sad knowing that she needed that kind of affection just to get her through the night.

Susan at this stage had no idea what I was up to, even though I had, in theory, done nothing wrong. I had not even kissed Mandy, so was only guilty of holding her hand. Mrs Van Den Hauwe knew I had committed acts far worse than that since we had been together.

Things soon progressed and, before long, I was driving to the Smith household in Muswell Hill most days after training. They lived in a nice, four-bedroomed property which was nicknamed 'The House of Dolls', an apt name as Mandy, her mother and sister Nicola were all extremely attractive ladies. It was a house that Mandy had more than likely paid for as, despite what people think, she was quite well off in her own right due to the money she earned from modelling. She never discussed financial matters with me and I have no idea if she received a hefty settlement from Wyman. It was no concern of mine, as the less we discussed him, the better, was the way I saw it.

As time went on, I was spending more and more time with Mandy and eventually I fell for her. It was getting to the stage when Mandy was phoning me and asking me to leave home, to pack my bags and move in with her. It was crazy, as we had still, by this time, not even got close ... if you understand where I am coming from.

I decided one night that it was time to go home and tell Susan everything and that was one of the toughest things I have ever had to do in my life. My daughter Gemma was only two or three; I had actually taken her to meet Mandy and they got on brilliantly, which pleased me, even though it probably complicated matters and forced my hand slightly. Had Mandy not accepted that I had a child whom I adored, maybe I would have called time on the whole crazy relationship. As it was, she was superb with my little girl and that made me grow even closer to her.

So one fateful night, I went home, put my cards on the table and I don't believe I have ever been in a tougher situation. I simply sat Susan down and told her I had met someone else and was leaving her. It was the worst moment of my life as I walked out of the door and left Susan crying in the chair, cuddling my little girl. The image I have in my mind of that night still upsets me today.

I soon became a resident of the Smith house, which was a dream that soon turned into a nightmare. Within a few weeks, the press were on to us and the day it leaked was a dreadful one for me. From that day, it was over a year before my parents spoke to me and I got pure grief from everyone imaginable, apart from a few close friends who had known about the situation from day one.

I was not as close to the Spurs lads as I was with my old pals at Everton, so I felt lonely unless I was in Mandy's company. Had the likes of Sharpy or Howard been about, they would have taken me to one side and tried to talk some sense into me. As it was, everyone I was close to – the likes of Harold, Walshy and Teddy Sheringham – were involved with the Smiths as well. In a nutshell, I was knackered.

We slept together for the first time in the spare room of her house one afternoon when Patsy and Nicola went out shopping. It was more of a 'let's get this out of the way' kind of a situation for Mandy, so it was no great shakes. I did not know how bad her state of mind was at this time; she was scared and I was the mug who had fallen for her and was left to try and sort her nut out. I was the wrong man for the job.

As horny as Mandy looked, it was just not on. It was like going into a top restaurant and looking at the fantastic dishes on the menu, then being told the fucking kitchen was closed. I wanted her every time I looked at her, but it was not going to happen. I began to think that the girl was quite simply afraid of sex due to her introduction to it at such a young age.

My new life was a totally different ball game and I did not, like some, revel in the media attention we were getting. I was trying to concentrate on my football, trying to sort out what was fast becoming a bitter divorce, and also try and work out what was going on inside the mind of my new partner. To make matters worse, the press began to camp outside our home day and night and follow us every time we managed to leave it. Everywhere we went, we were besieged by the press. If we nipped out for a coffee, we were hounded; if I went for a newspaper or out to buy some cigarettes, I was followed; I absolutely hated the attention, but loved Mandy, so put up with it.

Mandy was used to the attention and she handled it brilliantly when we were out but, once back home, she used to go back into a shell and I began to realise that she had serious issues. I used to speak to her mother at length about my concerns, but all she said was I should do my utmost to keep her daughter's spirits up. She was genuinely concerned about her poor health and state of mind.

Mandy used to love making me look beautiful and would spend hours applying make-up to me and plucking my eyebrows; it was something that kept her entertained. I went along with it to keep her happy, although I always ensured that I had removed all traces of mascara and lipstick before I set off for training.

I became friends through the Smiths with a well-known hairdresser called Lino Carbosiero, and was introduced to a completely new set of so-called 'jet-setter' friends. Like Lino, some were good, although some were not so good and some were pure mugs. Peter Stringfellow was one in the latter category as, from the first minute I was introduced to him, I thought he was a complete knobhead. He was the biggest attention-seeker I have ever had the displeasure of meeting, and would drop people like lead weights as soon as he had used them for his own means, as I found out myself after Mandy and I had split up.

His moment came when I went to his club with some of the Millwall lads and thought I would try a bit of queue jumping, given the fact I had always been treated as a VIP by Stringfellow. I walked past the waiting masses and informed the well-dressed doorman who I was. He pressed the buzzer and Stringfellow answered and, when the doorman told him who required special access, he said, 'Tell him to fuck off!' I had obviously passed my sell-by-date as I was no longer with Mandy or playing in the Premiership.

I went to celebrity hairdressing sessions with people like Vinny Jones and even on make-up and modelling jobs just to please Mandy. I began to get on with the press a bit better and stated to get invited on TV shows, although I never received a button for it as all monies went into the Smith account. One show I remember was with Chris Evans and in the sketch we did we had to lie in bed and have a chat about a load of old bollocks. Unbeknown to the watching millions, I was pinching his knackers under the covers trying to fuck the whole thing up, but Evans was a top professional and got through it without batting an eyelid.

After a year, we became engaged to be married and that

was the usual pantomime scenario. Susan had, by this time, begun divorce proceedings against me and things were getting a bit messy. She had a top lawyer, while I had my trusty pal Nick and some Spurs lawyers batting for me. I thought deep down I was on a hiding to nothing, as the break-up was not in any way whatsoever Susan's fault. I then had a tip-off that she had met a new bloke who was living in – on paper, at least – what was still my house.

Susan denied this, so I hired a private detective and got photo proof that this bloke was co-habiting with her. Eventually, we came to an agreement after months of haggling that we would sell the property via an auction, as I simply refused to pay for a house that she was living in with another bloke.

One day we were shopping in Harrods and Mandy noticed this stunning 3.75 princess-cut diamond ring which retailed at £55,000. She tried it on and it was the one she wanted, so we got a family friend to go to Belgium and buy the same stone and I had a jeweller make her the ring. It cost me £35,000 – a lot of money – but still £20,000 less than the now chairman of Fulham was trying to take me for. Although I had blown probably six months' wages on it, the ring did the trick and, months after we had first slept together, I got to have a second go!

The following morning, I opened the curtains and the vultures from the press were once again snapping away at me, so I opened the window and wished them a good morning as I was in a fine mood, having lessened my load, so to speak. One shouted up that he had been informed that

I had bought a ring, and asked me what the occasion was, so I replied, 'No comment!'

Later that day, we were refuelling the car in a local petrol station having collected the ring and, as I looked at her in the car, Mandy mouthed, 'I love you.' It was the first time she had told me that and I was thrilled, although thinking about it now, was it me or the £35,000 ring she loved?

Back at the house, the vultures were peppering me with questions about this ring so I said it was a friendship ring. Quick as you like, one shouted back, '£35,000 for a friendship ring ... are you feeling all right, Pat?' I turned to Mandy and asked her what she wanted me to say, so we agreed to come clean with them and I told them we were planning to get married. Within an hour, we were imprisoned in her home and it was impossible for me even to leave to go to training. The papers the following day were full of the story and I was upset that Susan had become involved, and was quoted as saying something along the lines of how it was amazing I had £35,000 to spend on a ring, yet was unable to pay for my own daughter to be clothed and fed.

We planned the wedding for the following year – well, Mandy and her mother did. I just went along with everything they said. There was no point in trying to have any say in the matter, it was the Smiths' day, not mine. Prior to the big day, Mandy treated me to a night at the Savoy. It was superb, the nicest evening we ever had together, until she told me that we were in the exact room that Wyman had taken her to. Talk about spoiling the moment!

I was not allowed a stag night as such; we had a joint hen and stag party in a pub near White Hart Lane. It was arranged by Patsy and Harold and about 150 guests attended. Towards the end of the night, Nicola was pissed and she lifted her dress up to me and gave me a flash of her knickers. As she did, I saw that her mother had clocked her and the stare she gave us frightens me to this day. If looks could have killed, we would have both dropped dead on the spot. I managed to blend in with the crowd, but knew that Patsy had marked my card big time.

Hello! had signed us up for a three-part deal, via Patsy, which covered the engagement, the wedding and the honeymoon. It was a sham, really, and I found it depressingly fake, but the money was crazy, even though as per usual none of it was destined for my coffers.

The day itself was stunning and, on 19 June 1993, we married at Westminster Register Office. Mandy looked like Cinderella and, as we left the initial ceremony, there were over 100 photographers snapping away, which I found scary. I knew I had jumped into another world, one eventually I found I could not cope with. We were given a police escort to the reception and there were all sorts of security measures in place to stop anyone taking photos as *Hello!* had exclusive rights to everything we did that day.

At the reception, I was thrilled to see my parents had turned up and brought Gemma with them, but soon I was despairing as Nicola asked me whether I'd be mentioning her mother in my speech. What speech? Nicola was horrified and set about writing one to get me out of the shit, for if I failed to give Patsy credit for making the day so special, it would turn out to be the shortest wedding on record.

I managed to get through it and everything went well. We had a dance and ate and drank well; it was a very pleasant afternoon indeed. Eventually, I asked Mrs Van Den Hauwe-Smith, as she had asked to be called, to join me in the bedroom for the customary night of wedding bliss, although I hadn't banked on us being joined for the duration of the night by none other than her mother.

It was at that precise moment when I truly realised that when I had uttered the words 'I do' a few hours earlier, that I had taken on the entire family, not just Mandy. By sleeping with us that night, Patsy let us know that she was not letting go, and it was a subdued night, to say the least. Had her mother been so protective during the early stages of her daughter's relationship with Wyman, maybe her state of mind would not have been so fragile.

The honeymoon was the same; we were put up in a stunning hotel but along came Patsy with her two little Yorkshire rat dogs Mini and Moochie. We never had a minute alone, and what disturbed me more than anything was that Mandy never once questioned her mother's reason for being with us and seemed to believe what was happening was quite normal.

Once we settled into married life, we looked high and low for a place to live, but Patsy always came and put Mandy off and it was only a matter of time before I began getting pissed off with the situation and hit the ale. Her uncle carried on as my drinking partner and was a mediator when we had relationship issues. He was a great bloke and would always try and patch up our frequent fall-outs.

On one occasion, he tipped me off that the girls and their mother were going out and I gained access to the house and proceeded to cover it from top to bottom with Mandy's favourite flowers, St Joseph lilies. There was not a square foot in that house which was not covered with the things and, as usual, I got the call that I could go home to kiss and make up. The following day, the story was in the paper and, as always, someone not too far from us had received yet another fat cheque.

With Mandy not being able to eat like most people, we rarely went out for a meal or even for a drink, so spent most of the time cooped up in the house with her mother and sister. When we did venture out, it was a media-orientated circus that had invariably been pre-arranged by her mother and the press. It drove me fucking nuts. On the odd occasion we made it into town, there was never a dull moment and always for the wrong reasons. One such night we were in Terry Venables' club Scribes and were enjoying a night with Vinny Jones, John Fashanu, Teddy and plenty of other players and so-called VIPs. We were also joined by plenty of hangers-on, whom we used to call 'The Gatherers'. In London, and especially in these places, there were gatherers by the lorryload.

I was introduced to bloke called Christopher Quentin, although I was later told that his name was really Christopher

Bell, but as far as I was concerned he was Christopher Who? No fucker knew who he was until the name Brian Tyldesley was mentioned. I was told that he was once an actor in *Coronation Street* married to a lady called Gail. Now if that was the best he could come up with, I was not impressed, so he began harping on about how he was now a party organiser in London. I was still not impressed and found him to be a bit arrogant and in your face, and he also had what can only be described as a couple of slappers with him who were sitting opposite Mandy and Nicola.

As the night went on, I left them and went to the toilet to come back and find Mandy crying her eyes out. I asked her what was up and she wouldn't tell me, so eventually Nicola informed me that the two slappers with Brian Quentin or Chris Tyldesley whatever he was calling himself had kicked off on Mandy for no reason whatsoever.

I went over and very politely said, 'Excuse me, but why have you upset my wife?' They looked at me like I had two heads and said that they had done fuck all, so I lost my rag and started giving them a mouthful as I knew they were responsible for ruining our night. Teddy jumped in to calm me down and was pulling me away, but I shouted to Mr big-time party organiser, 'What the fuck have you brought these slappers here for?'

Quentin jumped up and said something like 'Who do you think you are talking to?' so I told him I had no idea as he was a fucking hanger-on nobody. We went eyeball to eyeball before Teddy pulled me away, only after I had told Quentin that he was out of order littering the place with slappers, and eventually we left and went to the VIP lounge which was a place he was surprisingly not allowed in.

I went and found Terry and apologised, as he would have found out sooner or later that there had been a bit of bother, but he told me not to worry and that Quentin and the company he kept were often involved in that kind of thing.

Nearly everywhere we went, we had murder. We were in another club one night and both Nicola and Mandy had tiny dresses on which barely covered their arses, when some dickhead pulled up Nicola's as she walked past. It was well out of order, but it's something that happens all the time in nightspots when young lads have had too much to drink. I did not see what had happened until I saw Mandy fly into this large group of blokes shouting and swearing at them. I walked over and tried to calm things down, but Nicola joined in and, before I knew it, we were in danger of getting done in as the situation had turned really nasty. I managed to get hold of them and get them out of there before one of the dickheads did something stupid with the bottles they had all picked up. Even a trip to the shops would go pear-shaped, for if a member of the Smith trio were not treated like the queen, they would kick off and cause murder.

By now, Nicola was doing a bit of modelling herself; she was a very nice girl and one day I think I came close to cracking it with her. Amazingly, Mandy and her mother went out and left us alone in the house and I came out of the bathroom wearing just a robe to find Nicola standing against the banister wearing just a skimpy t-shirt and a pair of jeans with the buttons open, flashing the top of her knickers. I was paranoid that it was a set-up, but could not stop looking at her and she then asked me to do her a favour – wax her legs! She peeled her jeans off and lay on the bed and I'm there as horny as an old goat trying to concentrate on the job in hand but knowing that given the slightest encouragement I'd be on another job in seconds. I pulled the wax strip too slowly and she screamed and I think it brought us back to our senses as she quickly got dressed and we never dared mention that incident to anyone again.

I began to think our relationship was jinxed as there would be an incident of note every week without fail. One night, we were in bed and we were woken by a commotion of some sort outside the family home. I went out in my bathrobe to discover that a pissed-up driver had ploughed into a skip we had hired to fill with rubbish. I was supposed to have put cones and a light on it but had not bothered, and when I saw the state of the car my arse fell out. There was blood everywhere and I was soon joined by Mandy and the in-laws in their dressing gowns and slippers and they nearly passed out when they saw the carnage. Some locals managed to help the driver out and he legged it, leaving the passengers in the wreckage covered in blood. He did me a favour as the police never mentioned the lack of cones or lights, as they knew he had crashed because he was about five times over the limit.

To keep Mandy happy, I wasted thousands of pounds on expensive items of jewellery for her, including a solid gold cross that was encrusted with diamonds that cost me

£12,000. I also paid £5,000 for some bangles and bought her loads of other bits and pieces. One night, we returned from a rare outing and Patsy said she'd heard a noise upstairs a few minutes earlier. I went upstairs to find this huge black bloke hiding behind the curtains in our room holding a crowbar. I screamed downstairs for them to get out of the house and I flew down there to join them in the street. Within a minute, it seemed that every police officer in London had descended on the scene and the press were there at the same time.

I smelt a rat as a few weeks earlier I had been asked if I could help them out with a huge tax bill, which I was unable to do. Every piece of jewellery that was insured was taken that night, on the one night of the month that I was out of the house – strange indeed!

I agreed to stop drinking for Mandy and was even covered in nicotine patches as she tried to get me to stop smoking as well, but it was all a waste of time as, sooner rather than later, I knew she would tire of me and I was right. I was coming home after games and we just sat there watching TV without speaking a word to each other and, in the end, it just got boring so I'd go missing and hit the bars. I was chased by the police one night who suspected me of drink-driving and I parked up and ran into the house where Patsy hid me under stairs. I got away with it, but it was the only favour she ever did for me.

I learned a valuable lesson one day about how the Smiths worked when I defended Mandy in the middle of a heated argument she was having with her mother. In seconds,

Mandy turned on me, telling me never to interfere in family matters as it was none of my business. They then joined forces and attacked me like a pair of wild cats. That made me realise that the writing was on the wall; things were not working out as they should have done. We both knew we had made a huge mistake getting married and not setting up home by ourselves.

I had been with Mandy for about three years and we had slept together just four times. At this time, my career was affected by our relationship and I was no longer a regular at Millwall, never mind Spurs. I came home one day from training and went into the conservatory to see Mandy sitting next to her mother crying her eyes out. Patsy stood up and said, 'I think it is time you two had a break from each other!'

I argued the toss with her but she was adamant that I should leave for three months and then see how things panned out. It was a ridiculous situation; the best chance we had of working things out would have been for Patsy to have packed her bags and to have pissed off. I knew there was no chance of that happening so, reluctantly, I packed mine. I told Mandy straight that if I was to go I would not be coming back, and she just looked at her mother and continued crying. Her mother was ruling her life; I could see it but, sadly, Mandy couldn't.

During the initial three-month trial separation, I met a tennis coach called Vince Ranson at the local David Lloyd Centre and went to Brown's nightclub with him. I knew the owner, a nice bloke called Jake, who took us upstairs to the

VIP area. It was wall to wall with real celebrities and Chris Quentin was nowhere to be seen! I was introduced to an odd-looking gentleman who said he was 'Right Said Fred' and who bought us drinks; George Michael was in there and we had a fantastic evening. I had to get off when Jake's bird came on to me, which was a risky situation, so we made our excuses and left.

We ended up at another club where I was introduced to a lady whose opening line was, 'I have been told all about you and have been warned to stay well clear!' As it happened, she didn't heed the advice she'd been given and we ended up back at her place, although we never got up to much. I woke up in the morning to find she had gone to work and left the door keys with a note asking me to lock the door on the way out and post the keys through the letter box. I never knew her name or saw her again, but was told some years later that she was a well-known actress.

I ended up back at my mother's one morning after being on the piss all night with Ranson and the snake phoned Mandy from the flat and told her that I was fine and on the sauce all the time. We fell out over that and it soon surfaced that he was dropping me in it as he was trying to get into Mandy's knickers. I hope he had more joy than I did!

The trial separation ended in divorce and the papers and magazines had a field day as, no doubt, Patsy was on the blower the moment I had set foot outside the front door selling them yet another exclusive. One magazine at the time published the following article:

In 1993, Hello! *magazine trumpeted what sounded like the perfect union when 'the world's most romantic man' married 'one of the world's most beautiful women'. Over a spread of 17 pages, the nuptials of Pat 'Psycho' Van Den Hauwe, dressed like Spandau Ballet's sax player, and Mandy Smith, the former 13-year-old girlfriend and ex-wife of Rolling Stones bassist Bill Wyman, were covered in sumptuous detail. The former Everton full-back was portrayed in unrecognisably glowing terms and though ten years earlier he had been one of the hardest members of Birmingham City's notorious band of brawlers alongside Mick Harford, Mark Dennis and Martin Kuhl, here he was described as 'one of the world's top footballers' and 'a striker for Tottenham'. As all but* Hello!*'s regular readers pointed out, the only things he regularly struck were opponents' legs.*

But that apart, the magazine accurately captured the first example of a footballer's romantic bond with someone famous for being famous. A year later, Van Den Hauwe was toiling for Millwall while his bride picked up a coveted Rear of the Year award and another at-home piece in Hello!

Despite often denying their marriage was in trouble, they divorced a year later. At the outset, one partner praised the other for bringing sanity into their life; by the end, one was remarking how the other had brought madness to theirs.

I could not have put it better myself!

I was wide open to criticism and, although I expected it from Patsy, I was disappointed when Nicola began to have a pop in the press. In one such article, she was quoted as saying, 'I wasn't sad at the break-up. I'd rather Mandy got well than be with someone with his own problems.' My only problems were caused by living in The House of Dolls with those three nut-jobs!

Nicola's profile included: 'Claim to fame – sister to Mandy and ex-girlfriend of Teddy Sheringham'. That summed her up in one sentence. She went on to say how fantastic her mother was towards Mandy and was quoted as saying, 'Mum tried to slow things down between Bill and Mandy. He was wonderful to Mum, and she didn't see the danger signals. She was so ill that she did not know if she would live, and she saw Bill as someone who would look after her daughter.'

Now I admit 100 per cent to not being the best parent in the world, but come on! A 40-year-old bloke, worth millions, is looking after a 13-year-old girl, and you don't see danger signals for fuck's sake! Had he not been a famous rock star, but a bus driver or a bin man, would she have seen them then? Probably.

Nicola harped on about her mother's illness and depression, but does not say she was too depressed or 'ill' to sleep with Wyman's son Stephen, who was about half her age. Work this one out – had they all got married, Bill's son would also have been his own father's step-dad! That's how bizarre the situation was, and it was me who was burdened with trying to sort Mandy's life out when it all went tits up.

Is it any wonder I had my own problems, as Nicola put it?

Before we divorced, I had a call from Mandy asking me to meet her in the park near her house. I thought there was something seriously wrong, so I shot over to find that she just fancied a bit of rough up against a tree. It was the same story again a few weeks later when she asked me to get in her car. Twice in a few weeks after being starved for three years, that's how mad the situation was.

Our divorce was amicable; she asked for nothing as, by then, she knew I had nothing, as I was skint apart from my pension money, which she knew I could not touch.

A recent article in the *Telegraph* magazine entitled 'Famous for Being Famous', made me chuckle as it summed up the madness surrounding Mandy perfectly, stating: 'After splitting up from Wyman, Mandy became the occasional singer, occasional TV presenter, occasional model and full-time celebrity. In 1993, she married footballer Pat Van Den Hauwe, best known for hitting the bar, usually in the early hours of the morning.' The article finished with this classic line: 'Mandy has turned to God, the ultimate father figure. "He's important to me. I don't think he gets enough recognition for what he does. Look at all the lovely animals you can have."'

Ladies and gentlemen, I give you Mandy Smith, Mrs Van Den Hauwe Number Two, God's number-one fan. Very beautiful, but not the brightest young thing among his many creations.

Joking aside, I look back at that period of my life in horror. OK, I had a few laughs and lived the high life but wish, hand on heart, that I had not been in the wine bar on that fateful day when Amanda Louise Smith walked in. Between her and her control-freak mother, I almost ended up as crazy as they were.

15

FINAL WHISTLE AT THE DEN

Due to Ardiles playing silly games, my move to Millwall very nearly did not come off, but eventually the deal was rushed through and I was registered with minutes to spare. Had that deal not made the deadline, I would have walked from Millwall to Spurs and given Ozzie a good hiding. Although Millwall were not a top-flight outfit, I just wanted to play football and get away from a person who had apparently harboured a grudge for years, a man who was hell-bent on making me pay for one bad tackle and a silly comment made years earlier.

Ardiles did everything he could to cock the move up. Originally, he told me I could go on a free but, as I drove to meet Millwall officials on the Wednesday, I got a call saying that there was a mix-up and that Spurs wanted £100,000 for me and the deal was off. The following day, as I was about to return to Spurs, I was told to go back to Millwall as Ardiles had said I could now go for nothing as originally agreed. I got to the final stages of the move and was then told that Spurs wanted me to pay them £10,000 they claimed I owed them, with interest, or the deal was once again off. They were that petty they even demanded the money that day, sent via a taxi driver, before they would sign my release papers. I had no option but to pay it and coughed up the ten grand just to get away from the place.

As desperate as I was to play football, the money I was offered at Millwall was really poor and I think they were on to the fact that Ardiles would not let me join another Premiership club. That did not mean I was going to go anywhere for the kind of crap deal that was put before me and soon they realised that I was no mug and upped things a bit. They were still miles away from what I believed I should have been offered, but said that they could afford no more but would throw a motor into the equation. I told them I had a fucking car and wanted more dough. I was represented by Eric Hall, the 'monster, monster' agent who was very well in at Spurs until he fell out with some top clients and ended up out of the game. Eventually, I ended up agreeing to take a huge drop in salary, was offered a £20,000 car I didn't need and signed a three-year deal just fifteen minutes before the transfer window closed.

The following day, I drove to the training ground and a lot of the youngsters there could not believe that Millwall had managed to sign me; a few months later, they probably wished they hadn't. Mick McCarthy was very nice guy but I soon realised he was a tough bloke to play for. I sat there thinking I'd have a day of rest being shown around the facilities, when he just looked at me and told me to get changed and get training. He was right as I needed to get fit and, as soon as I got changed, was introduced to the lads who at once made me feel very welcome, which was nice after my year of hell at Spurs.

I made my Millwall début away to Charlton and what an eventful début it was. After just 14 seconds, I caused uproar when I elbowed a bloke called Shaun Newton and all hell broke loose. The Millwall fans went crazy. I had won them over in less than a minute! Luckily, the referee missed it but the game boiled over as tempers flared and eventually he sent off my new team-mate Alex Rae and a Charlton player for fighting, before booking me when I clattered their lad up front, Garry Nelson.

The game finished goalless and, at the end, a fight broke out in the director's box when the home chairman Robert Alwen was assaulted by a Lions fan. Welcome to Millwall!

I knew the chairman's name as he sadly tried to take me to court for the elbow on Newton and reported me to the PFA and Football League, saying my challenge was 'totally unacceptable' and the sort of thing 'football can do without'. Nothing more came of the incident and I was disappointed that some bloke in a suit watching from the director's box tried to nail me for a challenge via the courts, when everyone else had forgotten about it within five minutes of the game finishing. After just one game, Mick stood up for me, which was typical of him, as he was a very loyal man to his players.

I needed a couple of games to get match fit, was soon in the swing of things and found it easier to play after dropping down a league. I was an ex-Premiership player, had played international football and, for years, had been playing with some top-class players so had learnt a lot. I found it very much easier to read the game at that level, even though it was a bit frantic and the tackles a bit tastier, something I was more than capable of coming to terms with.

I was doing well for Mick when I got injured during a game at Bristol City. I went in for a tackle with City's Brian Tinnion and at once knew my knee had gone. I was carried off and I was told I would be out for weeks with knee ligament damage. I was depressed and hit the booze and soon fell out of favour at the Smith household and eventually left Mandy and moved back in with my parents on the Ferrier Estate.

Although my marriage was not perfect at Spurs, I was happy enough, but when I dropped a level I was out of the spotlight. Perhaps that wasn't to Mandy's or her mother's taste? Had Mandy ever loved Pat Van Den Hauwe, or had she just fallen in love with the idea of a footballer playing for a top club?

My split from Mandy was the beginning of the end for me, as I hit the booze and started hanging about with a gang of lads nicknamed 'The Five Ball' – myself, Keith Stevens (who was nicknamed Rhino), Alex Rae, Gav McGuire and Andy

Roberts were the original members, and our catchphrase was 'Fancy a quick half-hour?' After training, that was our code word that meant we were going for a proper session. Most of the time, I would be with them 'til late afternoon having a few beers and relaxing, then I'd go back home to The Watt Tyler to finish the day off.

One night, the lads phoned me from a boozer near Millwall telling me that Gav was blitzed and they could not shift him. So I drove over, picked him up and took him home, which was a big mistake. He lived in Bray in Windsor, a beautiful place full of beautiful women and nice bars. Gav was single like myself, and we had a field day there. He was banned from driving, so I used to spend a few days with him and he was an absolute diamond of a fella, 100 per cent nuts. He had a serious knee injury and was out for months but after we had been for treatment and a bit of physio, we used to go for a few beers every day, without fail.

One night in Bray, I met a bloke in a bar and he introduced me to Charlie – as in cocaine. It was the first time I had ever taken it and almost the last. The following day, we all arrived at training and a bloke from the FA came in and Mick McCarthy introduced him as a random drug tester from the Football Association. He informed everyone that the testers could come to any ground at any time and test any of us. I nearly shit myself and thought I was going to be banned after my first ever line, but the bloke just said his piece and went away without testing anybody.

At the turn of the year, Millwall were in second place and

in with a great chance of making it to the Premiership but, although our home form was excellent and we only lost one game at The New Den all season prior to the play-offs, we were poor on our travels. We finished third, nine points behind second-placed Forest and a massive sixteen points behind champions Crystal Palace, despite having beaten both of them.

During the season, I had lost my discipline and was not training properly. I could not be arsed going through the motions as I was not a first-team regular and was pissed off training with the reserves. We had a huge Cup tie coming up against Arsenal, but the problem I had was that Mick wanted me to fill in at left-back as his first choice was out injured. I had been playing well at centre-half so asked McCarthy why I had to be the one to be moved about to accommodate players. I was not a kid who was happy to play anywhere just to be in the starting line-up as I had done at Birmingham and wanted some stability.

A week before our biggest game of the season we were doing defence against attack set pieces and I was fucking about when Mick stopped the session and said, 'Are you gonna fucking train properly or not?' I told him I could not be bothered and told him to stick his reserve team up his arse in front of everyone and we had a few words before he said, 'Right, let's get this sorted … me and you behind the shed.' I realised I had been out of order and told him pack it in for fuck's sake, and we left it at that. McCarthy was a tough fella and did not give a fuck for anyone who crossed him. The incident was leaked to the local press and I will give Mick credit as he was quoted as saying, 'It was no big deal, I'm certain it's not the first time Pat has been sworn at and I'm sure it won't be the last time I'm sworn at either!'

Some years later, a bust-up Mick had with Roy Keane at Ireland's World Cup base received far more publicity than our set-to at Millwall, and resulted in Keane being sent home. People who don't know much about Mick would probably have put money on Roy if that row would have gone behind the shed; my take is they would have been betting on the wrong man.

After our disagreement, McCarthy went on to say that he understood my position and that I was in contention for a starting place against Arsenal. A few days before the game, we went out to Portugal to prepare for the Cup tie and I was involved in everything he organised. Mick was true to his word as I played in the game that we deserved at least to draw, but which Arsenal shaded 1–0. Despite being on the losing side, I played well enough to be awarded the man-of-the-match award.

Having buried the hatchet with the manager, I got back into the training and kept my place in the side for a few weeks. The team strung a few wins together and were pushing for an automatic promotion place when we met Leicester at The New Den, a side who also had a chance of going up. After half-an-hour we were down to nine men as first Terry Hurlock and then myself were sent off, both with straight red cards.

Although McCarthy defended us after the game and blamed our reputations rather than our actions for the dismissals, I think deep down he was pissed off with us as we were both seasoned professionals and had been a bit stupid with our actions.

So I was out of the side again and hit the booze and one day was with Gavin in the treatment room pissing about – nothing serious, a bit of swearing and basically acting like kids. Mick walked in and just sent us home, saying he did not want to see us behaving so unprofessionally at the ground in front of the younger players. Mick was losing patience and he knew I had given up the fight. He never went mad but the way he handled the situation let me know he was bitterly disappointed with how I was behaving.

Even though I knew I was doing myself no favours, I carried on going out on the piss with 'The Five Ball'. The truth of the matter was, I had got to the stage of my career where I knew I was on a downhill slope. I had joined Millwall thinking I would be a regular, having dropped a division. I felt that I would be able to compete with ease at that level, even if I didn't train as hard as I was supposed to. That was not the case as the league was very competitive and, although I had the experience to handle the best of the opposition players, my fitness was a problem. I could do 90 minutes, no problem, but it began to take longer to recover after games and knocks that would clear up after a few days seemed to keep me out for a couple of games.

When I was not playing or training, I hit the booze and spent more time in the pubs and bars than I did at the training ground, and some of the things we got up to were crazy. We used to play a game that involved standing next to a dart board with one hand on it while the lads threw darts at you. The idea was to get the darts between your fingers but we were so pissed we'd throw them like spears! You could not move your hand out of way as you would lose too much face. Sometimes all three darts would be embedded in your hand and we were forever going into training with them bandaged up. It was a stupid, idiotic game but we loved it. The locals in the pub looked at us like we were demented ... and they were probably right.

One night I was in a club talking to some bird with Rhino and another player when a midget of a bloke came up to me and was aggressively asking who I thought I was talking to. I swear he was only chest high to me, so I looked down at him and told him I was chatting to this lovely lady and to piss off and leave us alone. He then pointed out that the lovely lady was indeed his wife. A fight broke out and the bouncers dragged me and Keith downstairs while the midget laid in to me. We found it hilarious – he would have needed a step-ladder to headbutt me and we just pissed ourselves laughing.

As we got dragged down two flights of stairs, I was so pissed that I did not feel the pain from worst carpet burns I'd ever had. Outside, the bouncer asked if we wanted any more, but as it was apparent I already had a busted nose with blood pouring all over my shirt, I replied, 'No thanks, I think I have had enough for one night!'

We went back to our team-mate Andy Robert's house, who was a younger lad who still lived with his parents. The three of us crashed out in his bed and when his poor mother came into his room in the morning to wake him up she nearly had a heart-attack when she saw the state of us.

I was in and out of the side but was selected to play in the play-off decider against Derby. We lost 2–0 at their place and our chairman accused Derby of kicking us off the park, while Mick McCarthy called for the fans to get behind us and make the return leg intimidating for the visitors. He actually wrote a piece in the match programme saying, 'The Derby fans managed to make it a hostile environment for us up there and I know from experience that they cannot hold a candle to the Millwall crowd in this department.' He was spot on, as anyone who knows about Millwall and their fan-base will realise that the gaffer did not need to rally the troops, as even on a cold Tuesday night at a youth team game the place was as hostile as you could get.

By half-time, the game was over – we were 5–0 down on aggregate and I had suffered the embarrassment of scoring an own-goal. Our fans had seen enough and the scenes at the end were riotous, not intimidating, as Millwall thugs continually invaded the pitch and a couple of Derby players were attacked by unhappy locals.

Millwall were charged by the Football Association with failing to control our supporters in scenes they described as 'the worst crowd violence in recent years'. Our chairman was distraught and offered to resign, saying, 'Naturally, we are very upset by what happened. We had over 300 stewards, 200–400 police, a number of police horses and deliberately kept the lower north tier empty so there could be no possibility of conflict between the fans. We believe we took every possible precaution.' He could have erected electric fences and had moats around the pitch with crocodiles swimming in them for all the good they'd have done; Millwall fans are a different breed and not even the severest measures would have prevented them rioting that night. They took missing out on promotion to heart and, looking back, I was partly to blame for it.

We regrouped and went on a tour of Ireland for a week but I trained only once, stayed in the hotel, and went on the Guinness big time. At same time, Keith Stevens was still mourning the death of his father and was in a bad way and really upset, so we both comforted each other. I was depressed, as the reality of my life being in such as mess hit home and I remember that sad day like it was yesterday. I had hit a new, all-time low. I was so depressed I told Andy Roberts I'd had enough and was quite simply going to jump into the sea and drown.

Basically, I could take no more – Mandy, booze, drugs, it was all too much for me. I had been 15 years on the circuit and was back to square one living in the spare room of my parents and could not cope any more with the way my life was panning out. It was just too hard to take.

I went and knocked on Mick's door in a right mess and he was quality. I told him everything, even about the sniffing. He told me to go home and get right and that I had his full support. I told him that I thought that would be worse as I would be back in London on my own and knew I would go on the piss and score Charlie. At least I had the lads in Ireland, so he agreed I could stay with them, but I never trained and just carried on drinking, which probably made him think he was banging his head against a brick wall.

The club physio was quality, a great fella; I also told him everything and he asked me to go to his house at weekends to sort my head out, just to relax and get out of the way. That was stunning of him but, as always, I never took him up on it and carried on with the drink and drugs.

Eventually, he got me to go and see a psychiatrist, who turned out to be a complete fucking idiot. The fella was a proper old fart who was in his sixties and did not look interested in me, which at once got me agitated with him. He said he could recommend some medication that would help me and that I should come into the clinic in the morning for an injection, then back at night for some sedation medication. I looked at this pillock and said, 'How the fuck can I play on that medication, you stupid bastard? I need to be concentrating on my football and you're trying to numb my nut.' I just got up and walked out and the physio asked him to forward the bill to the club before following me after half-heartedly apologising for my outburst. I needed counselling, not a nut job; it was a complete waste of time and the scene was like something out of *One Flew Over the Cuckoo's Nest*. I needed answers as to why I was off the rails, why did I have to do everything to the extreme? This twat just wanted some silly cow to stick a big needle in my arse every morning and have me wandering round like a zombie all day before returning for some sleeping tablets at night! It was probably the biggest waste of an hour in my entire life.

With no answers, I carried on and got deeper and deeper into the drink and drug culture that was rife in London. I began to knock about with a bloke called Leroy and, one day, four of us were in a pub when about eight big geezers walked in. They took a good look at us and Leroy recognised them as West Ham heads. He went over to them and I was wondering why he was talking to them. A minute or two later, he came back over and said, 'It's all sorted, mate ... we can finish our drinks and leave, but must do so in five minutes.'

I couldn't believe it. 'You fucking what? No cunt is telling me where I can and can't drink.'

He was adamant that we had to leave, so we drank up and left. We went somewhere else and he told me that, but for the fact they respected him, we would have been done there and then. It scared me a little as I was never one for picking and choosing my watering holes and never really thought that I could be badly dealt with just for playing for another team. Of course, we had the odd row at Birmingham with Villa fans, in Merseyside with Liverpool fans and in London with Arsenal and Chelsea fans when I was at Spurs. This, however, was a level above that and Leroy put me straight that with West Ham and Millwall there were no limits and, despite being a player, not a gang member, I could be seriously beaten up just for drinking in the wrong boozer.

I played a game here and there but did not feature in Mick's plans, so over the Christmas period I went on a huge bender. One day, I was with some of the Millwall lads and we stumbled across a bar full of Arsenal players. I had the customary bird in tow and noticed George Best having a drink and was in awe of him as he was my boyhood hero. I took a deep breath and walked over and asked him would it be possible for me to buy him a drink. He was very polite but told me he had a drink already and thanked me for the offer. I noticed that he had a big, fresh cut over his eye with blood running down his face so had obviously been in a scrape of some sort. I got talking to the Arsenal guys and saw George leave about five minutes later, so I finished my beer and went looking for my bird who'd disappeared. I went up the stairs and saw Besty in the street outside getting into the taxi with two birds ... and one of them was mine! I thought, fuck me, he's done me ... but thought that if I was going to be done by anyone, then I may as well be done by the Best!

I met an old friend on the Ferrier estate called Tracey Brown and stayed with her for a while and it was from her house that I made the call to the club and asked to speak to the manager. Within a minute, I was put though to his office and he knew what was coming. I no longer wanted to mess McCarthy about; I was taking the piss and respected him too much to carry on, so said, 'Mick, I don't want to play any more. I have come to the end of my time here. I can't cope, I'm still on and off the coke and I'm out all night on the piss. Can you please get the club to pay me off? I don't want to be a footballer any more.'

He knew that I was serious and accepted it. I was not doing the club, myself or my team-mates any favours. Enough was enough. He agreed to sort it and I was paid off with £25,000. The whole conversation took less than five minutes.

I was driving around in a big Merc which was my own, not the one the club had given me – that had long gone back. However, I hadn't paid a button of the hire purchase agreement for months. A couple of days after leaving Millwall, some bailiffs found out where I lived and pulled in front of me, forcing me to stop, got out of the car and just said, 'Hello, mate ... sorry about this, but we need the car back.' They must have thought I was going to kick off as two big geezers got out, but the car was immaterial to me. I simply threw them the keys and joked I'd use the Underground from now on, thanked them very much and walked home to my mum's.

They looked at me in shock and were obviously expecting a lot more grief from me. What was the point? A car is a car; it was no big deal not having one in London as I just went out and about on the Tube from then on, which probably prevented me crashing the car while pissed up. Looking back, I used to drive in some horrendous states; I am ashamed of it now, I could have easily killed myself driving or, more worryingly, someone else, maybe some kids crossing the road. Losing the car at that time was a godsend.

I began seeing a girl in central London called Meredith; she was from Australia and very beautiful, but worked strange hours and wore skimpy clothes, if you get my drift! She was a very well connected and very exciting lady. I stayed with her for a couple of months in the middle of

London and visited all the top clubs and was, as usual, playing at being a rock star, but without having the wages to sustain it.

Somehow, I still owned my house and I used to use it now and again to crash out in if we were visiting that part of town. One day, I was with my old friend Tommy Hayes from The Watt Tyler, a truly great fella, who sadly died years later of a heart-attack. He was a legend of a bloke.

While we were crashed out in my house, the phone rang. I was amazed it was still connected as I had not paid the bill for months and was even more amazed when I answered it and heard the friendly tones of Howard Kendall. He told me that he knew I'd had problems at Millwall but asked if I'd like to start afresh and join him at Notts County? I told Howard I was finished, but he told me to get on a train and that he'd help sort me out. It was a sad conversation – I loved the man, but knew my time was up and, after a minute, we wished each other all the best and I thanked him for the call and carried on doing what I was doing. That was the day I knew that my career in English football was over, for if Mr Kendall could not talk me into sorting myself out, nobody could.

Thanks to my Australian girlfriend, I was now involved with some serious members of the London underworld and was doing way too much coke and booze every single day and night. I could go anywhere and do what I wanted thanks to the people I was knocking about with, but it was a world I knew I had to get out of and Meredith knew it, too, so she asked me if I wanted to go and live in Spain with her. Maybe if she had said Brazil or somewhere like that, I'd have gone. As I saw it, Spain would be like being in England with a bit more sun. In a nutshell, I couldn't be arsed packing a bag, so we split up and I had the maddest couple of months of my life as I blew £15,000 doing everything I should not have been doing all over London.

I was so mixed up I made a decision that could have had very serious repercussions on mine and other people's lives. By chance, I had bumped into the bully from my school days, Tony Merriman. Nothing had changed and he was in my face once again. I now realised he was jealous of me; even though I was on the slide, I had been pretty much as successful as you could get with Everton and Spurs, and he let me know that he was still not impressed with me. I replied in exactly the same way as I had done years before – I told him I didn't want any trouble, and walked away.

This time, however, instead of sitting in my bedroom, as I had done when I was a teenager, wondering how I could get him off my back and out of my face, I made a call to an individual who was very well connected with the people I was hanging about with. Within minutes, I had received a call back from a person unknown to me who asked me for information on Merriman and informed me that the problem would be sorted out for good. I knew exactly what that meant and I took a step back and called the whole thing off.

I am glad I did as, later on in my life, I realised what these people were capable of and, although I hated Merriman more than any individual on earth, including

Ozzie Ardiles and Patsy Smith, I did not hate him enough to want to read about him being found in a black bag on the banks of the Thames.

My old friend Nick Trainer sussed out what I was up to and he saved my life. He had to get me away from London and, one day, called me and asked if I fancied a little trip out to South Africa. I asked him if he was mad, as I thought the place was nuts. I was unaware of what it was like out there, apart from all the bad things I had seen on the news. He said he'd come with me and suss it out, that there was an offer on the table and that it was one worth taking a look at.

I had to decide which path to take – have a look at what South Africa had to offer, or to stay put. I spoke to my parents who were shocked at the measures I was prepared to take to get away from London, as they had no idea how low I was or what I was into. I went and had a bath and my mother came in and asked me to tell her everything, which I did. It was very emotional and she was crying but, eventually, agreed that I needed to get away if I was to have any chance of sorting myself out.

The following day, I phoned Nick and told him I would go for a week and see what it was like. Fifteen years later, I'm still there, so perhaps I'm in a good position to say that you shouldn't always judge a country by what you see on the news!

16

LIFE'S A BEACH

I hated the idea of going to South Africa. I thought that in days I would be kidnapped and killed, such was my ignorance of the place. Nick, however, managed to convince me that it was an opportunity worth having a look at, so off we went!

We had a nightmare flight out there; in a nutshell, it was horrendous and took us about 18 hours via Amsterdam and Johannesburg. We landed in Cape Town and, despite Nick trying to convince me to stay sober, I hammered the bar during the flights and was not in the best of states by the time we got our bags and made it through Customs. I was expecting a day in the hotel to recover, but we were picked up at the airport by a club official and driven straight to the training ground of the mighty Hellenic FC. So much for a fresh start. I was as rough as I had ever been and the bloke greeting us at the ground must have been hoping that it was Nick who they were signing. Sadly for the club and myself, it wasn't.

We were introduced to the manager, a bloke called Budgie Berne, a very well respected ex-pro from England. I had never heard of him, although within an hour I knew the ins and outs of his arsehole. Mr Byrne took great delight in telling anyone who would stay awake about how he was nicknamed 'Budgie' due to his incessant chatter on and off the pitch. He was not wrong about that. He went on to tell me about how he was one of the most skilful players of his generation but failed to win the honours that his rich talent deserved. His claim to fame was that he was the first Fourth Division player to be capped by England Under-23s – impressive indeed.

I will give the bloke credit – he must have been a half-decent player as his son David, who was also at the meeting, took over when 'Budgie' was getting his breath back. He told us that his dad made his full international début at Wembley in the 1950s and that he was the first Palace player to be capped by England since 1923. Had I been sober, I may have been slightly impressed; as it was, I was neither.

The meeting was like being in a room with Ant and Dec; once one shut up, the other would take over. Budgie went on to tell me that in March 1962 he signed for West Ham United for a fee of £65,000 which, at the time, was a British transfer record. Once again, I'll give the man credit where it is due, as West Ham were no mugs around that time, having the likes of Moore, Hurst and Peters in their side.

He carried on ... and on ... and on, telling us about how he helped the Hammers beat Preston North End in the 1964 FA Cup Final, and how he also went on to win 11 England caps, scoring 8 goals for his country, including a hat-trick against a Portugal side containing Eusébio. However, although he was included in Alf Ramsey's original 26-man squad for the 1966 World Cup finals, he was not one of the final 22 players selected and his international days were over. Thank fuck for that, as by now I had not been to bed for over 24 hours and was in danger of nodding off in front of his very eyes.

Byrne had been in South Africa since the late 1960s and played for and managed Durban City, whom he guided to League and Cup triumphs, and he told us that it was a fantastic place to live and that he would never return to England such was his fondness of the place.

I had only been there a few hours and thought, 'What a load of bollocks,' but Budgie was right and eventually what he told me that day all turned out to be spot on and, although we never really saw eye to eye during the time I played under him, I was saddened to hear of his untimely passing in Cape Town in 1999, aged just 60.

Having got the 'Budgie' Byrne episode of *This Is Your Life* out of the way, the club owner, a Greek gentleman called George something or other, set about selling the club to me. He told me that the likes of Alan Ball, Gordon Banks and even Bobby Moore had played for Hellenic and that they were a great club who could attract all the top players who were coming towards the end of their careers in England.

I was impressed – if Hellenic were good enough for England's World Cup-winning legends, surely they were good enough for Pat Van Den Hauwe? I wish I had been sober enough to ask the Greek owner how many games they had played for him, as once sober I made a few enquiries and I was informed that the names mentioned had indeed played for his club, in a one-off exhibition match when they had all finished playing professionally.

Eventually, I was handed a contract which in my inebriated state I would have signed there and then. To be bluntly honest, I was that pissed I'd have signed a valentine card for Patsy Smith or a get well card for Ozzie Ardiles! Luckily enough, Nick was on the ball and it took him hours to get it through to them that there was no way I was signing such a shit contract. Eventually, the owner said they would pay me 5,000 Rand a month, which was about a grand. On top of that, I would get various bonuses and accommodation, as well as the best car the club had to offer. They were sorry they gave me that, as it was written off within a month as I struggled to come to terms with the fact that the locals insisted on driving on the wrong side of the road.

I signed for three months with a view to a much longer deal if I did the business. It was not great money but decent for South Africa as it was a cheap place to live. I thought that I would piss it, as the standard was so poor. However, I did not take into consideration the time it would take me to adapt to the country and climate. It was horrible at the time, we were smack in middle of their winter and it was cold and continually pissing down and, although I tried – albeit not very hard – to adjust to my new surroundings, I just could not settle.

I was put in a hotel and, as is the case with hotel life, you either vegetate in your room or hit the town, and that was a no-brainer for the likes of myself. Soon I had Nick in tow as he was basically on holiday for a week now that the deal had been signed and sealed. Within a few days, we had our first fall-out as, like I have done all my life, I met a lovely young lady and fell for her. Nick was trying to get me back to the hotel as he knew that I could not go missing during my first week at the club. During the silly argument that followed, I kicked him in the balls and told him to fuck off as I was too old to require a babysitter. I was totally out of order and we fell out briefly before he returned to England, so I informed him that I was going home with him. Nick was a rock and persuaded me to stay and to see out at least the three-month contract I had signed. Taking his advice was one of the best decisions I ever made in my life.

With Nick gone, I was looked after by Colin Gee, who trained the youth team. He took me all over Cape Town looking for somewhere to stay, showing me all the options available and eventually I got a nice apartment on the beach front. Things were looking up. I found a nice little bar 50 yards up the road, run by bloke called Selwyn who became a very good friend of mine and who helped me settle into life in South Africa.

I was enjoying life except for the football, as from day one I found the training tedious. It was all this clappy-happy shite, dancing about, it was useless and embarrassing. We were training like Brazil but were sadly lacking in rhythm, never mind quality, so I started to do my own thing which pissed them off straight away. I played a few games but I was not doing well, I was struggling with my fitness, as I was on the beer and, along with not taking training seriously, I was found wanting when we played.

It did not help when I was sent off in one game for two elbow offences, although I would probably have got away with a yellow had those two incidents not occurred at the same time. Two players were on my back at a corner and I did them both in a split-second before realising the referee was just a yard away.

Eventually, Colin Gee pulled me to one side and said that if I did not play well in the next game I was on my way home, so I bucked my ideas up and trained hard for a few days. There was a top striker up against me that everybody was raving about, but I did him early on and we won. Another contract was put in front of me that I signed and everybody was happy, for a week at least.

Our next game was away, which involved a short flight, which was delayed for a few hours, so I clattered the bar at the airport and ended up losing my ticket. One of the club officials went mad but they eventually got me on the plane so I carried on drinking. The following day, I was summoned to the manager's office and he went berserk, telling me I was a disgrace and a waste of the club's money and if he had known that I was such a headache he'd never have signed me.

Deep down, I knew he was right; everything he said was spot on, but I was having such a superb time at night that his so-called bollocking fell on deaf ears. I simply told him that I had not lost my flight ticket on purpose and to chill out. I think he was probably expecting an apology – he deserved one – but at the time there was no way I would give him one so he fined me a month's wages. I lost the plot and turned on him, telling him to fuck off. He said all the fine money went into a player's kitty, but I accused him of trying to line his own pockets and we rowed for ages about it until eventually I said, 'Fuck you, fuck your club and goodbye ...' I walked out the door and that was that.

By this time, I had cashed in a pension from England was given a pay-off from Hellenic thanks to Nick's negotiations, so I had about £60,000 burning a hole in my pocket. I was now looking to enjoy South Africa and had a considerable amount of money to do it – a dangerous combination. In local currency, I had over half a million Rand and, believe me, was I going to make the most of it!

Despite only being in the country a few months, I had made some great friends, so even though the reason I had arrived in Cape Town – to play football – had gone west, I had no intention of flying back to England. As I lived in a club apartment, I had to find somewhere to else to stay as I was no longer on the club's free housing list, so I set about finding myself a nice place to live in the thick of the action. I was introduced to a couple who were friends of Colin

Gee's, who told me that their brother-in-law had a huge house in an area called Hout Bay which was a truly beautiful place to live. It sounded too good to be true and there was indeed a problem – the bloke who owned this magnificent property was gay.

But regardless of the bloke's sexual preferences, I needed somewhere to live, so I went and met him. I got on with him within minutes of us being introduced and, although 100 per cent camp, Kevin was a very intelligent and funny individual. I put him in the picture that I was straight and had no interest in men, and he promised me that he understood the situation and that all he wanted from me every month was the rent. The situation was better than I could have hoped for as he informed me that he was an air steward. This meant he obviously travelled frequently, leaving me as the sole occupier of this huge house situated in one of the most sought-after areas in town.

We shook hands and, to celebrate our new arrangement, he asked me to join him for a drink and, as expected, he took me to a gay bar … or, in his words, 'a poofs' bar'. I am not being homophobic – it is what Kevin and his mates called it when in my company. In fact, to this day, he is still in my phone contact list under Kevin the Poof!

I was a new face on the block and, as soon as I entered the bar, all his mates were trying their luck with Kevin's new lodger. One by one, they were told in no uncertain terms that if they did not keep their distance, they would get a dig. Eventually, the penny dropped and they started asking me to go out with them to other venues as a mate, not a potential target. One club we frequented was called The Bronx, totally gay, but an amazing place.

My new home was nicknamed 'The Queen's House', but it was more like a mad house. Every night Kevin was home, there was a party to commemorate something or another as he would celebrate the opening of a tin of soup! He had wardrobes of women's clothes and quite often, after a few too many drinks, his mates would ask me to dress up with them but one glare was enough to let them know I was a jeans and shorts man.

The place was a millionaire's hang-out and was where I was introduced to a property developer called Mr K, a top fella, who lived in Durban. He had business interests worldwide and was forever in Cape Town setting up all sorts of deals. He owned two Harley Davidsons and a Dodge Viper and we would bomb about the strips on the Harley and pull birds left, right and centre. We became huge friends and he introduced me to a lifestyle that made my time in Birmingham, Liverpool and London seem like Sunday school outings.

His home in Cape Town was a superb apartment in a place called Buckhoven, 20 minutes from where I stayed. Within weeks of meeting him, we were coked off our heads and visiting all the top night spots, basically living the high life. Every night we were bang at it, bird after bird, huge amounts of cocaine and even larger amounts of alcohol. I would drink six pints of lager then hammer a bottle of vodka.

Every day was manic; it was an amazing time of my life.

I was living like a rock star and, although it was fantastic, it obviously had its drawbacks.

During this period, Budgie got sacked as manager of Hellenic. Colin Gee took over and was soon on the phone pleading with me to rejoin them. Under normal circumstances, I would have laughed at the offer; I was having the time of my life, but needed to be working to secure a visa, as every six months you had to fly back to the UK and renew it. My beef had been with Byrne, not Gee. He had helped me get a place to live when I jacked in, so it suited both parties when I agreed to rejoin Colin at the club.

With my visa sorted, I was back to the rock 'n' roll lifestyle and, although I gave it a month at the club, I ended up walking out again. I should never have gone back as I hated it there. Colin never tried to stop me; he knew I had bundles of money and was on the piss big time, as well as hitting the Charlie. It's fair to say we left by 'mutual agreement' – I told him I was fucking off and he agreed that I should.

Some months later, I had to fly home again to renew my visa and was shown a press cutting by a friend with the headline 'FROM SOCCER STAR TO BEACH BUM!' The story went on to say how I had fallen from grace and was now a drunken, womanising bum living on the beach in Cape Town. They were right on two counts, but I lived in a top gaff and I was extremely angry that people in the UK would have read the article thinking I was living like a tramp. Due to my experiences with Mandy, I still had some very good contacts in the press so made a few calls and, within an hour, was given the name of the person who had sold the story to the highest bidder ... Colin Gee!

Two days later, I was back on the plane to Cape Town and my first stop was Hellenic Football Club. I went straight to the ground, pushed past the security guards and walked into the middle of a training session with the first-team squad, stopping it dead. I looked at Gee and gave it him big time. I called him every name under the sun and let every single player know that the bloke was a grass. I also let them know he was a liar, as they knew where I lived and that, although off the rails, I was no beach bum. Gee was in a state of shock and was muttering that I had got it all wrong and that he had nothing to do with it. When I told him that I had spoken to the bloke who wrote the story, he just held his head in shame.

Colin later became the agent for Quentin Fortune, one of South Africa's most famous players, but received plenty of bad press, none more so than when he turned to opening up academies that were hardly run as they should have been. To this day, the man is well known in South Africa as one not to be trusted – and I, for one, can vouch for that.

17

IN LEAGUE
WITH THE DEVIL

Once again, my football career was over, so I carried on partying with Mr K in between his busy business schedule which meant more booze, more birds and, by this time, far too much Charlie. It got to the stage where I was going off with friends of friends to score coke in dangerous places. One night, we were that desperate for drugs we even went to a black township called Gugulethu. Now I went with these guys whom I hardly knew and, as we pulled into the garage where the drop-off had been arranged, my new 'mates' all pulled out loaded pistols in case the deal went pear-shaped.

I was shocked at first. We were only buying a quarter-of-an-ounce and I never realised that some dealers in the townships would shoot you for the money involved in such a small transaction. When we got home safe and sound, Mr K told me that I was a fool going there as it was a place where you could be killed and nobody would bat an eyelid.

I became very close to Mr K and began going to business meetings and the like with him and visited his home in Durban quite frequently. On one such visit, I had too much money in my pocket so spent a week in the Beverly Hills Hotel which cost me 10,000 Rand, which was a hell of a lot of money in those days. The reason behind it was simple – I had met and wanted the manager's wife, a very attractive lady who was also up for it. After days of getting nowhere, she ended up getting drunk with us one night and I managed to get her back to my room and it looked like my 10,000 Rand was a good investment, but she was so pissed she just crashed out naked on my bed and slept like a baby all night. I was gutted, but more so when her husband found out and barred me from the hotel.

A few weeks later, I was told that he was going to get me done in, but I wasn't going to be intimidated, so I went and met him and I told him to fuck off. I was once again out of control and did not give a flying fuck about anything. After six months, they split up and he moved back to the UK, so the next time I visited Durban I called her and we more than made up for her nodding off in my company on our previous date.

I was introduced to a guy called Costa who owned a Shwarma bar, imaginatively called 'Costa's Shwarmas'. It was a great meeting place and I bought my first gun from him for 2,000 Rand. I went to register it in a police station but was told I could not take it home to Cape Town as firearms weren't allowed on an aeroplane. So I kept it there with him and took it everywhere with me when I was visiting. By now, I was visiting often as the rock 'n' roll, drug, booze and bird lifestyle I was growing fond of was even better in Durban.

I had the most hilarious time ever when a member of the Millwall 'Five Ball' arrived in Cape Town but, as well as it being hilarious, he caused absolute murder. The ex-player – who I will not name for the sake of his reputation – called and said he was coming over to visit, so I agreed to collect him at the airport but, of course, forgot due to being on another planet. Eventually, he tracked me down and he was in a right mood until I took him out and introduced him to my new lifestyle. Within half-an-hour, he pulled a bird in this stunning bar overlooking the ocean and the locals inside looking out of the huge glass windows were treated to a bit of a show. Some were not impressed and the following day the owner pulled me to one side and told me that I needed to get a grip of my pal as that kind of behaviour could get him locked up if the police had caught him in action. I relayed the message but it fell on deaf ears, as this member of the 'Five Ball' gave even less of a fuck than I did. We would be on a crowded beach and I could sense he'd be planning something; the next minute he'd stand up, stretch, make a bit of noise to get attention, strip off bollock-naked and walk the length of the beach to the sea while blokes covered their birds' eyes in disbelief!

We went out one night with Mr K on a business meeting

with some of his opposition, a firm who had some right lumps with them. My pal took offence to something that was said to K, so he jumped up threatening the biggest one among them. He was rattling on about 'don't speak to my mate like that …' when, in reality, he had only known K for five minutes. I tried to calm it down but he was having none of it, even when I pleaded with him to leave it out. Eventually, this huge Chinese geezer told me to stay out of it and they took the disagreement outside where I witnessed the worst attempt at a straightener ever as every punch that was thrown missed its target. We all ended up rolling about laughing and went back in the bar as friends; even the business deal came off.

A few days later, another meeting we attended didn't go quite as well, so K handed me a .38 Special on the way home and said if this firm arrived at his home heavy-handed, be prepared to use the shooter. We were off our heads on Charlie and we went to the top floor of the apartment and were told to sleep on the balcony and keep watch in case this firm turned up looking for trouble.

We were lying there under this big blanket, shitting ourselves, and every time the wind blew or a cat ran through the garden we were up pointing this fucking gun in every direction. God knows what would have happened if someone had actually turned up – thank the Lord they never did!

We continued going to every pub, club and bar in town and all the bouncers wanted to kill my ex-team-mate as he was so disrespectful to them. It was a nightmare going out with him, but such good fun it was impossible to stay in. It was a crazy couple of weeks that I will never forget and, when he eventually buggered off back to the UK, it took me months to iron out all the problems he had caused. I have never seen him since and if he ever comes knocking on my door, my wife has been given instructions to tell him that I am out.

During my trips between Durban and Cape Town, I met a model called Candice who had a friend we called 'The Doc'. He could get Charlie that was almost pure; it was the best gear available, but that is the kind that gets you hooked, and sadly that was the case. I got heavily into the drug scene and stared going around with a gang of lads who all rode Harleys, and was introduced to a bloke called Steven Kentridge, an introduction that almost cost both of us dearly.

I was still having the time of my life, although I'd started to suffer paranoia due to the amount of devil's dust going up my nose, so I'd taken to carrying a gun at all times. I had bought my own .38 Special with an air trigger and I carried it religiously, loaded with deadly dum-dum bullets. If I ever had to shoot anybody, they were dead, as those things blew a hole the size of a football in you.

The times that gun almost got me into serious trouble were endless, but one of the funnier incidents came when I was sitting on the balcony of a friend's apartment overlooking Hout Bay. It was late one afternoon and I had left my cigarettes and lighter on the balcony, was as pissed as a fart, coming off the coke and, as usual, as paranoid as ever. It was a roasting hot day and I was nodding off on a sun lounger, when an almighty bang woke me up. I shit myself and thought I was under attack, from whom or for what reason I had no idea. Paranoia took over me completely, and I ran into the bedroom, got my gun and took a kneeling position behind the table ready to return fire ... only to see that my fucking cigarette lighter had blown up in the heat! I'll tell you what – it was incidents like that that got me thinking it was time to get off the powder. I could have opened fire and shot at anyone, given the crazed state of my nut.

A few nights later, we were driving to the strip in K's open-top convertible when we were held up by a couple in a motor going about 20mph in front of us. We had hot dates waiting in a bar, so K began tooting the horn and flashing his lights, but this old couple took no notice. So I pulled the gun from the glove box and – BOOM – blasted a shot into the sky. K nearly crashed, the car in front sped off and we never saw it again. He went off his nut as the gun should only have been kept in the house for protection purposes.

I kept the shooter in a calf holster and how over that period I never blew my foot off was a mystery. I was off my head on anything and everything and was always messing about with it. It really is a miracle I have still got both my feet and all my toes, and it's a mystery how I never ended up in jail when I was carrying the thing.

I never realised it, but the drugs and drink had hit me hard and I was a loose cannon. People will say I was always like that but, when I was on the Charlie, I was worse, a lot worse. Things came to a head when I loaned this Kentridge bloke 1,000 Rand – about £100. Kentridge was a black belt in karate and every time I asked him for this money I got nothing back apart from sly comments. I realised he was taking the piss but, despite it being a small amount of cash, I was hell bent on getting it back from him.

The situation came to a head when, one night, I was with a group of friends having a great time. A beautiful girl was sitting next to me, and she began rubbing my leg, before pulling away in shock and blurting out, 'What the fuck are you doing with that? You're a footballer ... what on earth are you carrying a gun for?' She was horrified and walked off.

Kentridge then walked past and, sadly for him, it was purely bad timing. The bar was in a busy spot, right opposite a main road and a frequently used footpath. I walked out and saw Kentridge sitting on a window ledge chatting to some mutual friends, so I went over and, for the umpteenth time, asked him for my money. He clearly didn't give a shit and said, 'Not got it.' He then slyly turned away and carried on talking to the crowd.

I'd had enough, so I said to him, 'How many fucking times have I got to ask you for it? You're taking the piss.'

Once again, he was blasé and said something like, 'Not much you can do about it is there? I'm far too quick for you, pal.'

I thought to myself that if we got into a fight, there would only be one winner. With his martial arts expertise, it was not going to be me, so I just turned around, put my leg on a stool and pulled the gun out. In front of all the punters and countless passers-by, I calmly put it about 6in away from Kentridge's head and said, 'Now then, Mr Black Belt ... you're not too fucking fast for this, are you? Now where's my money?' It was only a hundred quid for fuck's sake, and there I was, with my finger on an air trigger with the safety catch off, ready to blow his head off for such a pittance. I had reached a new all-time low and this guy's reaction would no doubt change the course of my life for ever. If he went for me, he was dead, no question about it.

Thank God he didn't. It was the strangest feeling I had ever experienced. Had a car gone past and beeped its horn, I'd probably have pulled the trigger and blown Kentridge's head off. He looked at me, horrified, and eased away in total shock, managed to get behind a tree ... and was off. To this day, I have never set eyes on him again and never did get my hundred quid back!

The incident was over in less than a minute but it was one that was to change my life for ever. I was one slip of the finger away from committing murder, from a life in prison; I was knocking on the devil's door, waiting for him to open it. That night, he was out and I escaped a life of hell.

I often get flashbacks of the incident and it horrifies me. Had the police turned up I would still be in jail to this day, but they didn't, so I put the gun away and went home. I didn't sleep a wink that night, and the following morning went to Mr K's and gave him the gun, holster and all the bullets back. I did not want to see, let alone possess a firearm ever again and, thankfully, that has been the case ever since.

I settled back to life at The House of Queens trying to behave myself and keep off the devil's dandruff, but started getting frequent messages left on the answerphone from an English guy called Steve Bailey. He was calling at all hours and every day for about a week and I began getting in a raging hump with the bloke.

Eventually, I spoke to him and he told me he had been over in South Africa for about a year and ran a football club called Wynberg St Johns, and asked if I'd be interested in signing for them. He explained they were a Second Division outfit playing in the Vodacom League, so I arranged to meet him at a bar on Camps Bay Beach.

It was a great meeting, we had a good chat and got totally annihilated. He seemed to be my type of bloke, so I agreed on my terms to go and have a look round and see if it was something I might be interested in. A month or so later, I went and had a look, and met Steve in the players' bar where he introduced me to club officials and the players alike but, more importantly, to a lady. We never knew it at the time, but she was destined to become my rock ... and Mrs Van Den Hauwe Number Three!

Carolyn de la Cruz worked for a courier company as a rep and knew everyone at the club; she was the daughter of Mr Dennis de la Cruz who became the first Leader of the Opposition in the House of Representatives in the South African Parliament in the mid-1980s during the Apartheid era. We were introduced and, despite her impressive background, I fancied my chances at once but got the knock-back and was gutted. Never one to give up, I met her a week or so later and we went for a nice meal but, once again, I got nowhere. So I bought her some flowers – not a bunch or a bouquet, a fucking shop full. I was carrying big money about and wanted to show her and everyone else that I was no beach bum!

I was seeing an English girl at the time and Carolyn knew in a round about way that I was attached to her, probably as the maid at the house had grassed me up. I was glad when it was time for her to return to London; so much so, I went on a bender on the day she was leaving. I hit the whisky and was in a dreadful state; I got so pissed that, when we arrived at the airport, I got out of the car, went to get her bags and collapsed on the road. She had to get me into a taxi and give the driver my address to take me home. I must have had alcohol poisoning, as I was in bed for a few days before I was well enough to collect my car and, for some reason, never saw the English bird again!

With the girl gone and time on my hands, I agreed to help out at the football club where I often met Carolyn and we got on great together. Around this time, I had a fall-out with Kevin at The House of Queens. It was something and nothing, but I ended up telling him to fuck off and he made a big mistake as he jumped up and in true 'bitch' fashion pulled my hair. From a kid to this day, I have hated that; all I could think of was the bully Merriman who always pulled my hair as a youngster, so I turned round and smacked Kevin. I should not have done it, but my hair is a no-go area. So he caught one on the jaw and ended up flat out on the living room floor.

I went and packed my bags, but Kevin had decided that I was going nowhere and locked all the doors and even the gates outside which were about 6ft high. I climbed out of the window, threw my bag over the gate, climbed over after it and said goodbye to The House of Queens. I'd had some great times in that house, it was a superb place to live. I lost count of the amount of women I'd entertained under that roof, but the time was right and I was out of there.

Carolyn had been to The House of Queens, so knew who I was living with and was not too shocked when I phoned and asked if I could stop with her for a few nights. Fortunately, she agreed and, on 7 September 1996, the day of her 34th birthday, I moved in with her and we are still together to this day.

A few nights turned into a few weeks, then into a few months, and eventually we became a proper couple. I still had the odd night out, but Carolyn knew all about my drink and drug issues and was a rock. I gave her a life of hell when I was coming off the drugs and the booze, but she stood by me and helped me through it. Had she turned her back on me, God knows where I would be today, I really hate to think about what may have happened to me had it not been for her.

As I was returning to normal life, there was still the odd punch-up and one cost me a few quid. For some crazy reason, I had bought a diamond earring and was in a club with Steve Bailey when I clocked this fella looking at me. I always remembered Sharpy at Everton forever trying to stop me asking people what they were looking at. He'd say, 'For fuck's sake, Pat, you're a famous footballer. People are bound to look at you!'

However, in Cape Town, I was nobody famous, so I got it into my head that this bloke was looking for trouble. So I walked over and asked him what his problem was. Before I had finished my sentence, he had landed about half-a-dozen punches on me and I was in a heap and my earring was missing! Steve Bailey took me home and Carol said, 'Why is it that every time you go out you get into trouble?' I had no answer for her so decided to stay in more often!

Carolyn's sister was a model and we used to go to events she was appearing at and, at one such show, I bumped into and made my peace with Budgie Byrne. It was at a huge horse racing event called J&B Met. I shook hands with him and we had a good old laugh about the bad old days. When I heard he had died a few years later, I was really happy that I had squared things off with the man. May he rest in peace.

With my head now sorted, we decided to settle down and, in March 1997, we bought our first property in Plumstead, Cape Town. I used the last of my money, which was about 70,000 Rand, for the deposit and played for Wynberg St Johns who were in the Second Division at that time to help pay the mortgage. Later that year, after intense interrogation, I married Carolyn at Home Affairs in Cape Town and we celebrated our marriage with a party on 26 December 1997.

We dabbled in the property market and bought and sold

a couple of houses, one of which was stunning, that was paid for when I sold all my Everton and Spurs shirts, as well as other memorabilia in 1999. I got a decent price for them and dealers were pleading with me to sell my medals, but I decided to keep hold of them as they were all I had left from my time in the game. Sadly, it was not long before they, too, went under the hammer.

Things were going well but, in September 2001, Carolyn changed jobs and the struggle started when the companies she worked for changed her contracts. I had finished playing and could not land a coaching job, and I ended up maintaining gardens for family members to earn some money as we could not make the mortgage repayments. My medals were my last hope but, before they could be auctioned, we lost the house, which was really sad as we had worked so hard to keep it and loved living there.

We had to live in rented accommodation for a couple of years but, just before Christmas in 2003, Carolyn was headhunted by another courier company and there was hope for us again. In the new year, I finally managed to sell all my medals and we bought property in De La Haye, Bellville, Cape Town, and settled down to a normal life again.

I dabbled in some media work and was asked by ex-Manchester United 'keeper Gary Bailey and Terry Payne, who hosted a popular TV show, whether I'd like to join them on it. I was offered decent money to appear, but told them to shove it as I had totally fallen out with the game. When I look at the likes of Alan Shearer and Gary Lineker today, and hear what kind of money they command for talking bollocks, I think maybe I was a little too hasty making that decision.

We then embarked on a business venture which cost us everything we owned and almost ruined our lives. In December 2004, Carolyn was approached by family members who managed a very successful costume jewellery business hailing from the UK. She was offered a fantastic salary that, when topped up with the commission structure, was very lucrative. I was also given the opportunity to earn a reasonable wage assisting in the business. No written contract was in place as we 'trusted' the family and fell for it big time.

Things were going so well we decided to renovate our property and Carolyn also bought a new vehicle that would help us in the running of the business. We were far too trustworthy as the building contractor conned us out of 100,000 Rand and we could not recover a cent. We did not think we would need to get legal people in when we gave him the money, as he had been recommended to us by family friends. We then had a serious cash-flow problem, so had to tap into Carolyn's credit card to complete some building work just to get our home to a habitable in condition.

Within a year, Carolyn had increased the business to almost five times the expected amount and that was when the trouble started. She was looking forward to a good commission payout to settle our debts, but the family changed the commission structure that had originally been offered, again verbally. They argued that the payout was deemed too excessive, even though it was correct to the nearest cent. We tried to come to an amicable agreement, but she was told to 'take or leave' the new offer that was now laid out in a written contract. This contract was totally contradictory to the original verbal one and it divided the family. Carolyn went into a deep depression, mainly due to the financial struggle we were in, leaving us with no option but to sell our incomplete dream home.

We were forced to approach yet another so-called friend who was in the property selling business and, within 24 hours, he had a buyer. We sold all our household furniture, barring our beds and some personal effects, for approx 100,000 Rand, to get the creditors off our backs, and rented again while the house sale went through. After a few months, we were concerned that we had been given no information from the estate agents regarding a transfer date and we were running short of money to pay the rent.

The rental agent was very understanding and she asked us to obtain the proof of the sale of our property. It was then that we discovered that the estate agent selling our property was running an illegal scam and we were lucky to get our investment back. By this time, the market was in decline and we eventually took a massive knock on the new sale which did not even pay off our mortgage or other debts.

We ended up moving in with a friend who ran a guest house and, as neither of us had jobs, we took to picking up guests from the airport as well as doing some tour guiding in order to earn enough money to pay our way. I had gone from earning thousands a week and from appearing on

Match of the Day and in *Hello!* magazine to running an illegal taxi service and acting as a bogus tour guide in the space of just a few years.

Things picked up when, out of the blue, Carolyn was offered a job by a previous employer and the salary at least covered the rent and small monthly accounts, allowing us to rent a house in a beautiful area. Through all of the above, I have tried to find work and it was very difficult to cope with the stress and frustration. My pension helped each year but I am always looking to find a job offering a steady income. The stress got me to go on heavy drinking binges which almost destroyed my marriage and I am grateful for Carolyn's love and patience. Amazingly, she stuck with me and we have been married for almost 15 years.

Another major plus was when South Africa was given to chance to host the 2010 World Cup finals as, all of a sudden, there were many people from the UK and Europe taking notice of what was going on over here. Within months of the announcement, there was a flood of ex-players and football people trying to make inroads within the country. One such person was David Howells, an ex-Spurs team-mate, who, through a friend, asked me for a meeting. I never thought he was good company, so I blanked it, and he returned home telling everyone I was a drug dealer. Thanks!

One person I was happy to hook up with was another ex-team-mate, Trevor Steven, who is a very successful agent in the UK. I have for a couple of years been looking to send local players abroad, but have already been let down badly when I had a great chance of concluding a deal with a British club for a player named Teko Modise. The mandate was not signed by the owner of his club, called Orlando Pirates, which prevented him from moving to the UK. I tried again but was only given five days to get a visa by the UK company, and it was not long enough as the player was on international duty and my first major deal fell through by just one day.

That instance is typical of the way things are over here. It is hard for players to get deals suitable to all parties, because as soon as a club shows an interest in a player, the price seems to escalate. So far, I have not earned a penny from the agency due to red tape and greedy owners in South Africa, despite the profile of the World Cup.

Hopefully, things will change. I will not give up as easily as I did when my playing career went down the pan, as I am determined to repay the faith my wife has shown me and am no longer a quitter. I'm keeping myself active and play for the over 40s and, just two months short of my 50th birthday, suffered Cup heartache once again as we were beaten in a Regional Cup Final. I also do some charity work for an organisation in South Africa that looks after the street children.

Despite being let down badly over here myself, I am always happy to do anybody a good turn ... well, almost anybody! I say 'almost' as a couple of years ago I was called by a gentleman called Peter Du Toit, the owner of *Soccer Laduma*, a well-known South African magazine, asking me what I thought of a certain Mr Ozzie Ardiles. It emerged that Ajax Cape Town were thinking of talking to him about a coaching position at the club. After what I told Peter about him, he then called John Clemetre, owner of the interested club, and told him my views on Ardiles ... who did not get the job.

I sincerely hope, from the bottom of my heart, that it was my views that cost him that job!

18

UNSUNG HEROES

Two years ago, I was sitting in the garden, enjoying the South African sunshine, when I received a phone call from none other than my old drinking partner Graeme Sharp, who was calling on behalf of Everton Football Club ... inviting me to attend a dinner.

'Fuck me,' I thought, 'they must be short of guests if they have to invite an ageing ex-full-back who hasn't set foot in the place for nearly 20 years to sit round a table with them for dinner.'

Sharpy went on to explain that it was a reunion to celebrate the 25th anniversary of the club's greatest-ever season, and I was obviously an integral part of the original line-up. I explained to my old mate that it was highly unlikely that I would be able to attend as, unlike him, an ex-player who had stayed involved in the game and saved a few quid over the years, I was on the bare bones of my arse. And there was another minor issue – I no longer possessed a passport!

Graeme explained in greater detail that the club were prepared to fly me over and put me up in a hotel for a couple of nights if I'd agree to attend, so I told him I'd run it past the missus, try and get myself a passport and let him know. I then received a call from a Mr Andy Nicholls who introduced himself as a Sports Promoter. He told me he was mates with Sharpy and that Graeme had mentioned I was thinking of attending the reunion dinner. He then said that if I did come over, he could get me some work at some smaller dinners and introduce me to a few autograph dealers who, he claimed, would pay me decent money to sign memorabilia for them.

I thought this bloke was winding me up – why would anyone want me to sign a few pictures or shirts? Why would people want to pay to sit in a room and listen to tales of my time at Everton? Andy assured me that it was no wind-up and I agreed in theory that, if the club would sort my flight out to the main function, that I would meet him there and discuss some of his ideas in more detail.

I managed to get myself a passport, the club sorted my flight and, during this time, I kept in touch with Sharpy and Andy who both tried to convince me that the fans at Everton would be happy to see me and that I could also earn a few quid while I was back in the UK. I was unconvinced; it was years since I had played for Everton and, although I had a great relationship with them in the mid- to late 1980s, this was 2010, a new generation of fans were now watching the team and I thought they idolised superstars like Tim Cahill, not ex-pros like myself.

I'll be honest and admit that I was worried that nobody would even remember who I was and that I would look a fool at the events. At one point, I thought of backing out and letting them down with some excuse. That was not me, so I nervously caught the flight as arranged and set off to meet my old team-mates and fans – if any turned up.

I am so glad I made that trip, as there is a reasonable chance that it could have turned my life around. It was years since I had flown and the flight from Cape Town to Amsterdam was uneventful; that was the only part of the trip that was, though. We landed at Schiphol Airport and I followed the crowd through passport control and out of the arrivals lounge and, within a minute, was out in the streets of the Dutch capital! I was like a first-time tourist and it took me about half-an-hour to explain to the security police that I should not have left the building but gone to another terminal for my connecting flight. Eventually, they believed me, and I was allowed back in and shown to my departure gate like a little lost child.

I landed in Manchester and, after a few minor hitches, checked in at the Hilton Hotel near the Albert Docks in Liverpool city centre. The place was unrecognisable to me as the docks I remembered was a run-down area full of dodgy dealers and street corner pubs; the place now looked like a little London, it was superb.

One by one, the lads arrived – Sharpy, Howard, Bails, Inchy, Peter Reid, Trevor Steven … until there were about a dozen of us doing as we had done all those years ago when we played together, talking bollocks and getting pissed. It was like I had never been away!

It was a night I will take to my grave; we had a superb time and I was thrilled to have been given the opportunity to attend. On the day of the major event, the rest of the squad arrived, although it was disappointing that Kevin Ratcliffe, Neville Southall and Andy Gray were unable to attend for one reason or another. I was especially sorry that Andy could not make it due to Sky TV commitments. He was at a game in Germany the following day and sent his apologies, but Germany is only two hours away, tops. I think if he knew what kind of a night we were going to have, he'd have told his bosses at Sky to sort it for him. Either way, he was sadly missed, as were Ratcliffe and Southall.

Still suffering from hangovers, we were transported to the venue, a superb arena a few minutes' drive from the hotel and ushered into a private area for some club photos. After about half-an-hour, a bloke who I thought was Howard's minder came into the room with my old gaffer, and Sharpy introduced him to me as the Sports Promoter Andy Nicholls. Within seconds, the Everton security bosses were over and politely asked Andy to leave, and then Sharpy explained a bit about my new agent and it was colourful stuff to say the least. As Kevin Ratcliffe was not in attendance, a club official asked me if I'd lead the team into the main arena and take the Cup Winners' Cup with me.

I'm a shy bloke, but it was too good an opportunity to miss, so I happily agreed.

What hit me next still brings tears to my eyes. The doors were opened, 'Z Cars' began playing and every one of the 2,000 guests rose to their feet to greet 'The Boys of '85'. If I could bottle that moment and keep it for ever, I would. I nearly backed out of the trip thinking nobody would know who I was; I was wrong and was mobbed from one end of the room to the stage in scenes that money simply could not buy. The warmth and affection shown to me and the lads that night was truly heart-warming. We were treated like gods by an adoring public; it was awesome, truly awesome.

The night came and went. I was asked to go on stage and say a few words, but was unable to. Anyone there disappointed by my lack of participation, please accept my apologies; I couldn't take to the stage for any other reason than I was too emotional. I had been away too long, I had never said goodbye and had I gone on stage that night, I would have broken down in tears, such was the effect the initial reception had had on me.

I was due to fly back the following day but, after Andy had sold me a few of his ideas, the club kindly agreed that they would extend my stay and I was given another week to enjoy the kindness and affection that only Evertonians can give to their former players. I quickly checked out of the posh hotel – they are nice but are not for me – and I was soon settled in my old friend John Smith's house a few miles from town. I then began catching up with mates in drinking holes I had not had the pleasure of visiting for far too long.

I was so lucky that, on the Saturday, Everton were at home to West Ham and I was a guest on the pitch at half-time where, once again, the reception I was given brought tears to my eyes. I visited lounges, met the fans and numerous ex-players and, to a man, every single person I met made me realise that I was a member of a truly remarkable family called Everton.

During the week, I attended a few question and answer nights at various supporters' clubs and pubs and was amazed at the reception I was given. I signed so much memorabilia that my right hand had not been so sore since I was living with Mandy Smith! The night before I was due to fly home, I went to a function on the Wirral that was jam-packed and I was sad to say goodbye to everyone. I had been treated superbly but left knowing that it would not be too long before I was back.

When we met, Andy had given me a copy of his own autobiography – *Scally* – which, after a few chapters, explained why the Everton security guards were not too keen on him. He also told me that a publisher he knew would love to have a chat about the possibility of putting my story into print.

As I mentioned during the introduction to this book, I had previously written my memoirs with a media friend in South Africa, but the completed manuscript was not really what I wanted, so it never saw the light of day. I wanted my autobiography to be as colourful as my life had been, and was convinced by Andy that it would be if the people he knew were involved in its publication.

Within five months, I was back in the UK and did a mini-tour of sports evenings while spending every day working on the book. Once again, I had a great time as John, Andy and the Bennetts made sure there was never a dull moment for the duration of my stay.

One day, I was taken to meet Frank Bruno and my old mate from London, Nobby, joined us for the day. Nobby was a highly-respected member of the Krays' firm in the 1960s and had more tales to tell about fighting than Frank did, although his did not involve gloves and boxing rings.

To cap it all, we spent a day in London when I met up with my beautiful daughter Gemma and went on to meet my old boss Terry Venables. Tel is a very busy man but took time to meet myself and Andy with my old pal Nick Trainer, when he offered to help in any way he could with this book. I am not ashamed to say that when I left that meeting, I had a tear in my eye, such was the affection and respect that Terry showed me that day.

Once again, I took in a game during my trip and was one of many who had no doubt left their seats and were in the bars around Goodison when Mikel Arteta scored the injury-time equaliser against Manchester United.

So I left and flew back to South Africa knowing I would be back soon, as the book deal was sorted and we had a release date to aim for. I had been treated so well that I felt I needed to let people back home in Cape Town know that I was part of such a fantastic family, so the day before I departed, I booked an appointment in a tattooist's and proudly had the slogan 'Nil Satis Nisi Optimum' etched deep into my skin across the top of my back.

The launch of this book looks like it will coincide with the anniversary of the last time Everton won the League Championship. It is hard to believe that it's almost 25 years ago since that crazy day in Norwich when my winning goal clinched the title. So much has happened to me during that time, but it's a moment I think of every day of my life.

How times have changed – I can't believe that Everton are now a club that struggles to compete with the likes of Stoke and West Brom in the transfer market, when the likes of Liverpool, United and mega-rich Chelsea and Manchester City can go out and buy any player who takes their fancy.

I'm not one for pointing the finger at certain individuals, but surely there are people out there who would buy such a fantastic club? I was only at Everton Football Club for five years and, although I have the utmost respect for the fans of every club I have ever played for, I see myself as an adopted Scouser and a true Evertonian. I hope that, after reading this book, you can understand my reasons for leaving, a move that I still, to this day, regret.

The late, great Alan Ball, a true Everton legend, was once quoted as saying, 'Once Everton has touched you, nothing will ever be the same.' He is right – only people who have been part of this superb club and forged a relationship with you, the fans, could understand what Alan meant. I have and I do, and I know now that, from the minute I walked away from Goodison Park, football was never the same. I thank you all from the bottom of my heart for buying this book but,

more importantly, for allowing me to be a member of this
very special family.

The Everton family ... my Everton family.

Epilogue

BOYS DON'T CRY

On Sunday 27 November 2011 I was feeling good! I'd just finished my daily gym session and was sitting outside a bar in Cape Town drinking fresh orange – yes, fresh orange, no vodka in it! I was admiring the fine scenery and thinking about how my life was back on track when, like so many people that day, I was hit with a bombshell. My phone went and I answered a call from Lynne Smith who gave me the tragic news that Gary Speed had taken his own life.

I never knew Gary personally, but like the majority of ex-footballers from my era I knew that when we were coming to the end of our careers the man was making a name for himself and was destined for the top. He succeeded and had a great career, and at the time of his death seemed to have turned Welsh football fortunes on the pitch upside down. That took some doing, believe me.

Lynne told me that Gary had apparently hung himself and I was shocked and saddened that a man who seemingly had so much to live for had taken his own life. The rest of the conversation was irrelevant and as soon as the call ended I wept. They weren't crocodile tears for Gary – like I said, I never knew him. I wept because the sad news reminded me that just a few weeks before I had been about to do the same thing – kill myself.

I'd thought about ending it all years ago, and you'll have read about how Mick McCarthy and a few of the Millwall lads once talked me out of jumping off a bridge into the Irish Sea on a pre-season tour. That was a cry for help; I was still playing football and although I was depressed that my career was coming to an end, I was still young enough to maybe make something out of my life. Even though at the time I was doing everything possible to fuck it up.

Now it was 2011, I was in my fifties, and I had been waiting eagerly for my PFA pension to mature. It would give me the opportunity to pay off my debts and maybe open up a business or something like that to keep me busy and earn a few quid to see me through to retirement. I'll be honest and admit that when I was playing I never even looked at tomorrow, let alone the future; I lived and played for the hour, not the day! I did pay into the pension fund, though, so I assumed that when the time was right I'd have a lump sum to kick-start a few ideas I'd put together.

When the cheque eventually landed, I was distraught. I'd heard about pension funds losing value but without going into detail what I got was heartbreaking. I did a few calculations and it didn't take Einstein to help me realise that I was floating down Shit Creek with no boat, never mind a paddle!

I gave up – threw the towel in, if you like. Enough was enough. I took the decision to commit suicide, but this time I didn't tell anyone how I felt. I simply went to the bank, where I cashed my cheque and paid some bills. With what was left I bought a crate of whisky, enough sleeping pills to send a hippo to the land of nod and a Stanley knife. Then I checked into a local B&B and began the countdown.

This was no cry for help; I'd had enough and could take no more. I was as low as I'd ever been – even after my playing days were over, even after all the shit with Mandy had ruined my life, even after I'd blown my last wages on cocaine. Getting that paltry sum of pension money had tipped me over to the point of no return.

I wrote a few letter to the people closest to me and decided that I'd have a week in the B&B, binge on the whisky, and on the Saturday night when the last bottle was drained I'd take the pills, use the tool and get myself out of the lousy existence I was leading. I had only myself to blame.

Things were so bad in my head that I was ticking off the days on the wall of the poxy bedroom I was crashing in. It may seem selfish – there were people who were probably worried sick where I was – but I'd gone, I'd lost it and nothing in my own mind could convince me I had anything left worth living for. I was beating myself up inside. The good times, the Cup Finals, the medals, the money, the birds and the so-called fame all seemed to be wiped out by the bad times. I once had everything, but now it was just me, the last two bottles of whisky from the crate, a load of sleeping pills and fuck-all else apart from memories. Most of them made me weep.

I was waking up, taking a drink, and sleeping until my next craving stirred me. Then the door came in and two men, who I owe my life to, dragged me out of bed, tidied me up and frog-marched me to one of their houses to begin yet another chapter of my madcap crazy life. Emil Brice and Hendrick Human both owned gyms in town that I occasionally used, and they had been looking for me since my wife had said I'd gone AWOL. Luckily for me they tracked me down with a day to spare; I had one bottle left and was one tick on the wall away from ending it all.

For days they kept watch, looking after me and talking to me. That was the important thing, talking. I'd tried to hide everything away; I was ashamed of myself and was forever beating myself up inside, but still I'd put on a brave face to hide how I really felt. They got me back in the gym and to this day I don't miss a session and am as fit as I ever was.

Thanks to Emil and Hendrick I am still here to tell you

how low I had fallen, how depressed I was, how lonely I felt. Sadly many people who may also have experienced these lows – including Gary Speed – are not.

If any good can come from Gary's death it's the fact that it seems to have raised awareness into how people who seem to have everything can still be prone to manic depression. I read in the *Daily Mail* last week that Dean Windass tried to commit suicide recently and I'm sure there are many other ex-players who, when they hang up their boots and the money drains away as quickly as their so-called friends, have also considered taking the most drastic way out there is.

I also read an article by Allison Pearson in the *Daily Telegraph* that tried to highlight how prone men are to suicide. The figures are disturbing.

Men are hopeless at depression, but they are terribly good at suicide. That is what the sad statistics tell us. One in every 100 deaths is the result of what Hamlet called self-slaughter, and the vast majority who die that way are male.

Hanging is not a cry for help. It's the opposite. Decisive, quick, resolutely masculine. An exit that brooks no argument, no pleas to think again. Small wonder [Gary] Speed's death has caused such widespread bewilderment and anguish. A distraught Alan Shearer asked, 'Why, Speedo? Why didn't you give me or one of your other close mates a ring if you were feeling so bad?' His agent, Hayden Evans, went so far as to assert: 'Gary did not suffer from depression and he was happily married.'

Whatever the specifics of the case – and none of us knows what really happened and why – there can be little doubt that Speed took his life while the balance of his mind was disturbed. Gary Speed was, by all accounts, a proud and devoted family man. Yet, in his final moments, nothing could reach him – not love, not fear, not the thought of the abyss of pain he would leave behind.

It's been pointed out that professional sportsmen have form when it comes to suicide. Some 2.7 per cent of Test cricketers have taken their own lives – more than two and a half times the British male average. In his autobiography, published earlier this month, Jonny Wilkinson summons up a rare candour and eloquence for a top sportsman when he confesses that his fear of failure and obsession with perfection caused him to harm himself off the pitch. Good man, Jonny. Hard to own up to such vulnerability in a game where the one rule you must never break is: Big Boys Don't Cry.

When I read that article I did cry, and as I see it there is no shame in that. I doubt it will be the last time I shed a tear, either, as I'm sure in the future there will be times when things get to me. I just hope I have good people around me and that I have the balls to open up and talk to them. That is all it takes to pull through – support and guidance from the people close to you. Those simple things could prevent those who love you having to live with the pain and suffering that's left behind if you reach the point of no return ... just like I almost did.